Praise for *Raising Up Good Stewards*:

Dr Black has given us a challenging manifesto for stewardship today, bypassing all the modern innovations and taking us straight to the source – Jesus Christ and his apostles and the early church.
– **Archbishop Makarios (Tillyredis) of Nairobi,** DPhil from Oxford University, Orthodox Church of Kenya

During my three decades in medical missions in Africa, I have observed that finances are one of the greatest sources of conflict. Drawing on several decades of experience working and teaching in Africa, Dr Black addresses the traps of financial dependency and prosperity theology which have weighed so heavily on the Church, offering instead a clear path to financial freedom and the liberation it provides for individual Christians and churches to be what God calls them to be.

With his background as a church historian and theologian, Dr Black carefully weaves a beautiful tapestry of insights from Scripture, the Church Fathers, and respected contemporary leaders in Africa who give successful church approaches to godly stewardship. His eye-opening explanation of tithing from scriptural and historical perspectives will reset your thinking.
– **Dr Tim Teusink,** teaching medical ethics in Africa with SIM France-Belgium

Written by a scholar who was formed and has served both sides – the Global North and Global South, as well as Eastern and the Western Christianity, this is a breath of fresh air when it comes to stewardship and the discipleship it demands.
– **Very Rev Fr Evangelos Thiani (ThD),** Senior Lecturer at Makarios III Orthodox Patriarchal Seminary, Nairobi-Kenya

Dr Black provides us with a timely and very relevant theology of stewardship. The luring power of the prosperity gospel seems to have robbed many churches and leaders of their dedication to God's vision and his mission for us. This book is a serious call to return to God's mission in all respects. The finances of the church should be under authority, not of ourselves as church or ministry leaders, but of God's actual mission for us. If we let go and make church and ministry finances subjected to God's mission, we will discover there are resources for what God has called us for. The book is a must read – and a must do – for pastors and other ministry leaders!
– **Dr Hannes van der Walt**, Projects Manager for the Association of Christian Religious Practitioners, South Africa

With vivid stories, Dr Black illustrates how to recognize misunderstanding and manipulation about money in the church, calling out dependency, the prosperity gospel, mismanagement, corruption, and abuse of power. He then outlines a practical approach grounded in the sacrificial example of Jesus Christ to build a lifestyle of stewardship.

Pastors and congregational leaders concerned with the spiritual and financial health of their communities will be grateful for Dr Black's keen observations as a teacher, historian, and seasoned pastor who in his own life has "learned the secret of facing plenty and hunger, abundance and want" (Philippians 4:13). This makes his message truly authentic and gives it transformative power.
– **Very Rev Dr John A. Jillions**, author of *Divine Guidance: Lessons for Today from the World of Early Christianity*

Using excellent Kenyan examples, Dr Black reinterprets Christian prosperity within biblical perspective. I recommend it to not only teachers of the word but also to all Christians who honestly desire to see the church steward the world within God's parameters.

– **Rev Dr Julius Kithinji**, Lecturer and Head of the Department of Theology, Philosophy, and Biblical Studies at St Paul's University, Kenya

Raising Up Good Stewards identifies the real problem undermining good stewardship. It shows how institutions can break away from the culture of dependence and the fear of curses used by some preachers to extort resources. It also explains why believers ought to give. You want to share these lessons with members of your church, Bible study groups, and government policy makers.

– **Rev Dr John Michael Kiboi**, Author of *Assurance of Salvation* and Senior Lecturer in the Faculty of Theology at St Paul's University, Kenya

JOSEPH WILLIAM BLACK

Raising up good stewards

God's people using God's money for God's glory

Raising up Good Stewards: God's People Using God's Money for God's Glory
Copyright © 2021 by Joseph William Black.
All rights reserved. No part of this publication may be reproduced, distributed, or transmitted in any form or by any means, or stored in any database or retrieval system, without prior written permission from the publisher.

ISBN 13: 978-1-59452-777-7
ISBN: 1-59452- 777-6

Published by Oasis International Ltd.

Oasis International is a ministry devoted to growing discipleship through publishing African voices.
- We *engage* Africa's most influential, most relevant, and best communicators for the sake of the gospel.
- We *cultivate* local and global partnerships in order to publish and distribute high-quality books and Bibles.
- We *create* contextual content that meets the specific needs of Africa, has the power to transform individuals and societies, and gives the church in Africa a global voice.

Oasis is: *Satisfying Africa's Thirst for God's Word*. For more information, go to oasisinternational.com.

The author and publisher have made every effort to ensure that the information in this book was correct at press time and disclaim any liability to any party for any loss, damage, or disruption caused by errors or omissions, whether such errors or omissions result from negligence, accident, or any other cause. However, if you feel that your work was not accurately cited, please reach out to us at info@oasisinternational.com and we will make every effort to review and correct the book where required. Furthermore, any internet addresses (websites, blogs, etc.), telephone numbers, or the like in this book are offered only as a resource. They are not intended in any way to be or imply an endorsement by Oasis, nor does Oasis vouch for this content.

Unless otherwise indicated, all Scripture quotations are from the New Revised Standard Version Bible: Anglicized Edition, copyright © 1989, 1995 National Council of the Churches of Christ in the United States of America. Used by permission. All rights reserved worldwide. https://nrsvbibles.org/

Scripture quotations marked (NIV) are taken from The Holy Bible, New International Version® NIV® Copyright © 1973, 1978, 1984, 2011 by Biblica, Inc.™ Used by permission of Zondervan. All rights reserved worldwide. www.zondervan.com The "NIV" and "New International Version" are trademarks registered in the United States Patent and Trademark Office by Biblica, Inc.™

21 22 23 24 25 26 27 28 29 30 BPI 10 9 8 7 6 5 4 3 2 1

Contents

PART ONE: GOD'S IDEAL, OR OUR IDEAS?
1: Called to Be Faithful Stewards 11
2: Dead End Number One 21
3: Dead End Number Two 29

PART TWO: WISDOM NOT TO BE FORGOTTEN
4: Should Christians Tithe like in the Old Testament? 45
5: What Jesus Said about Money 63
6: After Jesus: Stewardship in First-Century Christianity 79
7: A Great Cloud of Witnesses 95

PART THREE: HOW STEWARDSHIP ACTUALLY WORKS
8: Leading by Example 113
9: Building Trust and Integrity 125
10: What Local Church Stewardship Looks Like 143
11: Changed and Called 155

About the Author 179
Acknowledgements 181
Endnotes 183

PART ONE

God's Ideal, or Our Ideas?

CHAPTER ONE

Called to Be Faithful Stewards

All over the world, people care about money – a lot. From sunrise to sunset we hustle to get money and dream about what to do with it. We buy books and attend seminars and watch videos, hoping for answers from successful businesspeople and financial experts.

When we in Africa look outside our doors, we see things that should not be. Taxpayers' money and donors' aid disappear into corrupt pockets and offshore bank accounts. Bribery affects everyone, down to the traffic police officer and the public transport conductor. Too many people seek leadership positions not to serve people, but to enrich themselves and their friends at everyone else's expense. Recently I was stopped at the same police checkpoint for the 13th time in the space of a year. The officer checked my insurance documents and licence carefully before asking me for a contribution for his "lunch" (a bribe). When I invited him to join me for lunch at the university where I teach just a few kilometres away, he suddenly lost interest and waved me on.

Sadly, even a church can lose focus and prioritize fundraising for buildings and projects over serving needy people. From the tin shack sanctuary down the road to the worship palaces of media superstars, many churches are lost when it comes to stewardship.

How much time have we spent considering what Jesus wants us to do with what we have?

Many of us believe we know what the Bible says about money. We put a little bit in the offering basket to fulfil our duty. We may even give the 10 per cent tithe we believe God commanded in the Old Testament. Perhaps we are convinced that God wants to bless us with prosperity. "If I have enough faith and give to the church," we tell ourselves, "God will move the financial mountains that block my way to the life I deserve."

> How much time have we spent considering what Jesus wants us to do with what we have?

Perhaps you are honestly struggling as I was. I always understood that I should give something to the church where I am a member. The church leaders where I attended complained that we were in a financial crisis because members gave so little to the offering. So, I asked the board chair if the leaders had a vision for what the church should be doing, had produced a budget, or accounted for the money the leaders spent. They did not do any of these things. I was shocked.

I believe that we are in the midst of a stewardship crisis:
- in our own lives
- in our churches
- across our continent
- even around the world.

If we could solve this, we would have more than enough resources to tackle the rest of our problems. Our problem is not a lack of resources; the problem is our misuse of them. The Yoruba of Nigeria have a saying that, "The wealth that enslaves the owner isn't wealth." The people who live in big mansions behind walls and electric fences are often living in prisons of their own making. More money and more things have promised a lifestyle that seemed so attractive. But more stuff cannot plug the gaping hole of meaning in their hearts. Lives based on accumulation get hollowed out. We were made for relationships, not for pursuing wealth and power.

As South Africans say, "money can't talk, but it can make lies look true". When we are not good stewards, we think we need to take from others to get what we need. False forms of Christianity are about what I can get and not so much about what I can give. Many cultures on our continent value sharing and community, although the Western form of Christianity emphasizes the individual, rather than our social responsibility to care for our neighbour.

Have we forgotten that God's first call on us and our congregations is to be good stewards of what he gives us?

Created to Steward

We human beings were created to care for God's creation. After creating everything else: "God blessed [humans], and God said to them: 'Be fruitful and multiply, and fill the earth and subdue it; and have dominion over the fish of the sea and over the birds of the air and over every living thing that moves upon the earth'" (Genesis 1:28 NRSV-A).

This earth is not ours – God made it. But he gives us the task of watching over and taking care of the creatures and the earth for him (Genesis 1:28; 2:15). God has created us with the job description of managing his creation. As we do this to the glory of God, we reflect his image.

Jesus talked a lot about stewards, especially the difference between good ones and bad ones. In Jesus's day, a steward was a slave whom an estate owner put in charge of managing his affairs. Today, we might picture a man who works in a big city but owns some land in the village. He wants to invest in farming as a side business, while he lives and works in the city. So he hires a farm manager and entrusts him with the resources to oversee the day-to-day needs on the farm. The manager has responsibility over the farm and thus has a powerful position. But he is still a hired worker.

Similarly, the stewards Jesus knew and observed may have had great responsibility for managing property and other slaves, but they were themselves still under the authority of the landowner. Their whole purpose was to serve the master's will.

We were created to be stewards – the farm managers – of God's creation. This is the astonishing message of Genesis 1–2. Everything we have, every shilling or naira or dollar, every relationship and opportunity that comes our way – this is what God gives us to steward.

Greedy Stewards

However, humanity failed to steward God's creation. Genesis 3 tells how Adam and Eve disobeyed God's command not to eat from a tree, and the tragedy that resulted. They were not content with being *made* in God's image. They wanted to be god-like themselves. They misused the authority God had given them to exercise dominion. When God confronted them, they refused to accept responsibility. Adam blamed Eve, the partner God gave him. She in turn blamed the serpent – ironically, part of the creation she and her husband had been asked to steward. Adam and Eve fell from fellowship with God and with each other.

All humans now share the consequences. Created in the image of God, we are still capable of much that brings God pleasure. But too often we follow the example of our first parents and abuse our authority. God called us to love him, love others, and care for his creation. Instead, we think of ourselves first. We compete with each other, lying, stealing, and killing to plunder creation for our own selfish desires. Our rebellion has bled into the whole fabric of the creation we were intended to manage for God's glory.

Rescue

But God himself decided to come into our broken world and do something incredible. Jesus came as a human to restore our relationship with God and others. He showed us how to obey God and live unselfishly. He showed us how to forgive each other – even people who hate us. By his death on the cross and his resurrection from the dead, Jesus opens the way for us to experience forgiveness and restoration in all of our relationships, and through us he has begun the process of re-establishing God's kingdom in this world.

Jesus saves us and restores us to who we were created to be. We were made to love God with all our heart and to love our neighbour as ourselves. When we know God loves us, we can love each other. When we repent for our sin, God begins to change our selfish hearts. Salvation reconciles us with God and the people around us.

Jesus also calls us to reclaim our original job description as stewards of God's creation. Salvation means living out our original purpose to use God's gifts for his glory. He invites us to join him in his mission to restore the world, becoming part of God's kingdom right here and right now. We begin to sacrifice our resources, our time, and our abilities to God to use for his glory.

Here is an example: Jane came from a small village, but she was a gifted student and worked hard. She dreamed of becoming a doctor to help people. After completing medical school and all her training in her country, many of her classmates left for Europe or America where they could make a lot of money. But Jane felt God had called her to serve in the rural areas she had come from. Her friends thought she had lost her mind. But she knew God had given her all her training and opportunities. She was determined to be a good steward of it and bless others.

A New Creation

A Swahili saying recently caught my attention: "To run is not necessarily to arrive." Many people are very busy, busy trying to succeed, busy being religious. But given all the effort, one wonders why so little change happens around us and in our own lives. But God's purposes never change. What God values remains as true today as it was yesterday. His goals are clear and have been clear from the beginning. God's goal is to restore his original plan – that his creation would glorify him and that the people he created in his image would steward his creation.

God's people, whom God is saving, become the means of God's grace for those around us. We are the beachhead for the invasion of God's kingdom on this planet. How we respond to God's love to us in Christ will be mirrored by both our response to our neighbour and the creation around us. It calls us to embrace our part in God's big story about stewardship:

Creation: Stewardship is what God made us for.

Fall: Almost every destructive problem we face stems from abandoning our calling to steward.

Rescue: Through Jesus, God saves his world and restores us to the stewards we were meant to be.

New Creation: Our eternal calling is to be stewards in God's kingdom.

Eventually, God will fully save us from the destruction and death caused by our rebellion. Like God intended in the Garden of Eden, he will live with his people, and "death will be no more; mourning and crying and pain will be no more" (Revelation 21:1-5).

God will "create new heavens and a new earth" and bring us back to life there (Isaiah 65:17). Creation will be restored so that even animals will be at peace with each other (Isaiah 65:25).

Just as stewardship was our job description in the Garden of Eden, stewardship will be our job description in the New Jerusalem. God's chosen people will build houses, plant vineyards, and "shall long enjoy the work of their hands" (Isaiah 65:17-23). We will live forever as image-bearers of God. God will make all things new in Christ, resurrecting and restoring his creation.

> Just as stewardship was our job description in the Garden of Eden, stewardship will be our job description in the New Jerusalem.

Although this will not fully be a reality until Jesus returns, in the meantime God calls us not just to come to him, but also to be stewards in this place. As we do, we become part of God's answer, God's means for saving his world. What could be more important?

God is breaking into human history right now, to reclaim this place and these lives for his kingdom. In individuals and communities, God is raising up stewards who reflect his image and proclaim his glory. These give us hope that it is possible to be better stewards of what God has given us.

A Tanzanian Steward

One of these new stewards is a friend of mine who distributed veterinary supplies to retail shops in rural Tanzania. He met corruption at every step: importers, government inspectors, wholesalers, and local vendors. He had to pay so much under-the-counter money that it seemed impossible to stay in business. He grew angry at the corrupt system.

Then he heard a simple sermon. It was not about how to get the success you want from God. Instead he heard that God was setting him free, giving him the power to live for God, and freeing him to love others. He began to view himself as the Lord's, and that all he had was now the Lord's. In response to God's goodness, he realized he needed to hand everything over to God, including his business. He offered himself to God to use however he chose.

My friend began to talk with his suppliers about the bribes they requested. Some were angry and defensive. But others were bothered about the web of corruption that had trapped them all. They began to find ways to avoid the bribes and kickbacks that characterized so much of the business. Even with those who maintained the old ways of doing business, my friend developed a reputation for honesty.

Because he no longer paid bribes, he passed on the savings to his clients, which they often passed on to their customers. He also rethought how to use his income. Before he became a Christian, he had avoided religious giving because he didn't trust those who handled the money. But now he noticed that he had the means to meet serious needs around him. He intervened in that widow's life, this orphanage, that church's feeding programme, that girl's tuition.

He did not draw attention to himself, but he made a difference in a growing circle of people. He became known as a generous man. The more he gave, the more he seemed to have. His family always had enough. He became a real disciple, living out what Jesus told his disciples when he sent them out to preach: "Freely you have received, freely give" (Matthew 10:8 NIV).

A Church of Stewards

African congregations are also becoming good stewards of the grace and resources God blesses them with. In a certain village church outside Kenya's capital city, Nairobi, church leaders constantly fought over money and demanded that church members give more. But they never produced a budget or informed the members how they spent the money. Two powerful men on the board were found stealing from the offering, but no one removed them from their position.

Instead of fighting with the leadership, a group of families decided to form a new church and leave the corrupt leaders to themselves. The new group determined not to cry for outside funding, but to depend on themselves and the Lord for everything they needed. They would be transparent and accountable about how offerings would be handled. Their new pastor would be paid a living wage, so that his family would not fear poverty. In return, the pastor would avoid temptation by having nothing to do with the offering or the church accounts.

Excited to be part of what God was doing, the members eagerly gave their funds, time, and skills. They met in a local school. Then they found a piece of land and within a couple of months they raised enough money among themselves to purchase it. There the church built a temporary structure without having to hire a contractor. Everyone helped. By the time the structure was finished, the church had grown from 80 to more than 200 regular attenders.

The church leaders were open to members' ideas for new ministries. Soon the church had budgeted support for missionary work in a remote corner of the country, begun a programme helping women in the church start their own businesses, and regularly supported their denomination's seminary.

As the church raised funds to construct a large permanent place of worship, they decided to match their giving with funds to build a school for disadvantaged children in their local community. Even though it was an immense amount of money, both the leaders and the members felt God's call. They decided not to accept money from outside sources or take loans.

The congregation, now 400 members, gave generously to the weekly offering because they knew their giving was safe from corruption and was making a real difference. It took two years, but the church raised the money for both the school and the church building. What had been a field of maize became a beautiful sanctuary and a primary school for poor children.

Over a thousand people attended the first service in the new building. The community had always been branded as poor and told that they would never accomplish anything. This church filled their neighbourhood with hope by their inspiring example.

Several years later, the new sanctuary is now full every Sunday. The leadership has a new vision for a ministry centre and a hospital since healthcare is difficult to access in their area. The congregation gives toward the work with a generosity unimaginable before, even enabling them to purchase a large piece of land next to the church. This is what practising stewardship can do!

In this book we will learn how to be godly stewards like my salesman friend and the village church. We will discover the Bible's call to be good stewards, from the Old Testament to Jesus. We will be inspired by how the early church lived out Jesus's teachings. My prayer is that you hear Jesus call you to trust him with all you are and all you have.

If you do, I know you, too, can experience the joy and blessing of stewardship. You can learn how to live out God's call for you. You can become what you were created to be. But be warned. This book will revolutionize the way you look at what you have and what you choose to do with it. It will challenge you to listen to what the Bible says about resources in a new way. If you will dare to take up the challenge, your finances, work, and relationship with God might never be the same.

CHAPTER TWO

Dead End Number One

At the end of a Sunday service in one church I know, a heated argument broke out between the choir members and the pastor. For as long as anyone could remember, the 20 men and women who led the congregation in singing had received travel money for their bus fares to and from church each week. But now, the parish was in a financial crisis. Major financial donors had returned to their home countries. The congregation was used to being supported by the generosity of one or two wealthy people. Now they were gone.

The members assumed, however, that the church would continue to support everything as usual. Nobody took steps to increase their giving. In fact, few people gave anything at all. Nobody asked how the church was doing financially.

So, the church had now run out of money. The security guards could not be paid, the water bill could not be paid, the electricity bill could not be paid, and the pastor's salary could not be paid. And the choir members could not receive their transportation money.

The choir leader threatened, "If you do not pay us, we will not come to services on Sunday."

These were not bad people. But the changing situation revealed that they were motivated neither by following Christ as his disciple nor by a desire to be good stewards of their musical gifts. Instead they were locked into a profound case of dependency. The idea that bus fare was part of their personal offering to the Lord did not seem to cross their minds.

What Is Dependency?

I tell this story not to embarrass or condemn anyone, but merely to illustrate a blind spot that can afflict any of us, regardless of nationality. The formal word for this is *dependency*, and it is a problem all around the world. It is like a dead-end street that looks promising at the start but in fact travels nowhere. Glenn Penner, who leads the Canadian segment of the ministry called Voice of the Martyrs, defines dependency as:

> It is like a dead-end street that looks promising at the start but in fact travels nowhere.

> A state where Christians as individuals or as a congregation allowed themselves to become reliant on another outside group or individual for financial and material means and, sometimes, administrative guidance, and are not therefore functioning in an indigenous manner ... The assumption by the dependent is that they cannot accomplish what God is calling them to do without foreign assistance, nor should they be expected to.[1]

Many Christians and churches across Africa struggle with the concept of financial responsibility. This is not entirely their fault. The absence of a theology of self-reliance and financial independence can be traced back to the beginnings of gospel efforts by European and North American missionaries.

Imagine what it must have been like, in the times of our grandparents and even earlier, when these pioneers arrived. People understandably viewed them as fabulously wealthy. Missionaries brought along fantastical technologies; machines designed to get them from one place to another. Missionaries had access to astonishing resources that enabled them to build what seemed to be vast palaces when compared to the one-room mud hut with a thatched roof that had been normal as far back as anyone could remember. Missionaries somehow were able to construct other buildings that they called churches and schools and clinics, buildings that had never or rarely before been a part of the local landscape. In the clinics, missionaries often handed out medicines that worked to heal those who were suffering.

Within a local community, there may have been grumbling by some who viewed these outsiders as a threat to the traditional way of life handed down from the past. But the missionaries got everybody's attention, with their comparative wealth, their access to technology, their medical marvels, and their willingness to engage and share with their neighbours.

The early missionaries and the people in Africa who came to learn the way of Christ usually had very good intentions. The missionaries sincerely worked to meet the needs of the local population, create good will, and then attract and establish a worshipping community. Many people were attracted to Jesus and the life-changing truth of his Word. However, in some places, becoming a Christian became associated with gaining access to resources. It was perceived as a way out of poverty into opportunity rather than a call to self-sacrifice. Some people sought positions of responsibility to exercise power and authority over the community, or even to gain access to wealth and property. Sometimes the men, women, and children attracted to the mission and its new community saw themselves as entitled beneficiaries of these opportunities rather than contributing members. "Church" and "mission" were something that someone on the outside did for us, rather than something we ourselves were and did.

Some missionaries were aware of the dangers of the dependence mentality they were creating among their church members, but they took a longer view of their efforts. They acknowledged that the first generation of converts might participate in their churches with mixed motives, and that some could be participating because of the material benefits and opportunities they perceived they would get. But the goal of the missionaries was to establish the church in the community as an ongoing presence and to focus on the next generation – the children – who through their participation in Christian education and school would become more "Christian" than their parents.

For example, a school might be started to educate the children of church members as well as to provide further opportunities to bring non-member families into the orbit of the church. This was not a bad thing. In fact, it was often very good and beneficial for the community as a whole.

But in actual experience, it didn't advance the understanding of Christian stewardship very well. Missionaries often found it very difficult to change the rules of the game that, after all, they themselves had established. All too often the relationship between missionaries and the churches they served had already turned into one of patronage, with the missionary dispensing the support, opportunities, and goods as the patron, and the church members receiving the benefits as the patronized.

Many stories could be told. Much history could be recounted. Mistakes were made by people with good intentions but not enough wisdom. At times, feelings were bruised. It should not surprise anyone that local churches receiving support from outside mission sources were not interested in letting go of this help and trying to make it on their own.

The Fruit of Dependency

One can understand that many people desire to better their lives, to provide for their family, to fit in with the regime in power and not cause trouble. The real cost of dependency is probably best seen in the life of the local churches themselves. In one Kenyan denomination, the leader (himself a missionary) repeatedly told the churches that he visited not to worry about contributing to the church's needs or to help with building a new church or school, because he would provide the funds.

To this day, hundreds of church members place something in the offering basket, but the amount would not be enough to provide a cup of tea for everyone after the service, or to pay for the pastor's petrol for his motorbike ride home. When asked why the congregation doesn't pay the pastor's salary when they obviously have the means to do so, the universal response is that it is the denominational office's job. "We can't afford to pay for his salary, or for anything," the thinking goes. "We are too poor."

I have experienced being jobless and not having a place to live. When I compare myself with people who have many material possessions, I feel really poor. But whether I have relatively little or relatively much, I still make choices every day about what to do with what I have and who I am. As a Christian, I'm called to follow Christ exactly where I am with what I have.

It is a great tragedy when any of us, from whatever background or level in society, falls into the assumption that Christianity is *something done for us*. Church is *something we attend*. In such cases, there is no ownership of the gospel, no sense of responsibility for the church's mission. We think Jesus has provided for our eternal salvation, but he is irrelevant to the way we steward our resources. We may call ourselves Christians, but we are not really Christ's disciples. Responding to Christ's call of being a disciple and a steward means I am still offering it all – however much it is – for him to use for his glory.

Finding the Way Out of Dependency

The way out of this attitude of dependency has not been easy. In some places, national events overwhelmed local experience. Sometimes armed conflict, or a change in government policy or regime forced the withdrawal of foreign missionaries with little notice or time to prepare local congregations for the shock. These local Christians were left on their own, as happened in Ethiopia, for example, after the Marxist *Derg* in 1974. Some who had been drawn to Christianity by their association with the missionaries and what they provided did not endure the transition and quietly followed the opportunities into a new Marxist identity. Others persevered, sometimes suffering imprisonment or other forms of persecution.

But was the true Christian cause diminished? Not at all. When Ethiopia emerged from 17 years of Marxist domination in 1991, there were many times more Christians than had been before the Marxists had taken over and sought to squelch them.

In other less violent places, mission agencies decided that their task was accomplished and turned over responsibilities to nationals. Of course, they attempted to train and prepare national leadership for the transition. But local churches and members who had gotten use to the largesse of Western missionaries suddenly had to make do with much less when the missionaries and their infrastructure disappeared. For many of the large mission churches across the continent, this transition was a very bumpy ride.

Many people did not expect the church in Africa to survive

without foreign support. The dependency mentality had assumed that African Christians had nothing to offer. But many African-led churches emerged out of dependency and found their stride as self-sufficient entities in the Christian family.

Today, Christianity is growing fastest in Africa! This should encourage us that outside help is not what will fuel our growth, but rather ownership and responsibility. Our generous God has blessed us with something to offer the rest of the world. Like the boy who offered Jesus his loaves and fishes or the woman who baked her last bread for Elijah, nothing is too little for God to use to display his glory and richly bless others.

"Do You Want to Be Made Well?"

I can spend a lot of time talking about where dependency comes from, about its effects, about how Christ teaches a different way, and about how dependency is fatal to genuine Christianity. But I will be wasting my time if there is no interest on the part of those stuck in dependency to be set free.

Sometimes we are afraid to let go of the way it has always been. If money is coming in from somewhere, why change it? Why take responsibility ourselves? It is risky to trust in God to provide in a new way. When I moved to this part of Kenya several years ago, I was given the task of teaching our leaders and churches about dependency and the way out of it. Over the next six months, I received zero invitations to teach about dependency at the regional or local level. I did, however, receive 12 invitations to be the guest of honour at a *harambee* (church fundraiser)! People were not really interested in breaking free of dependency.

> Many African-led churches emerged out of dependency and found their stride as self-sufficient entities in the Christian family.

When Jesus met the paralyzed man lying by the pool of Bethesda in Jerusalem, he asked a question that may have sounded strange: "Do you want to be made well?" (John 5:6 NRSV-A). He was, after all, the Son of God with full healing powers. Yet he wanted to know the man's frame of mind.

He is asking the same of us. Maybe you have been bent backwards in a posture of dependency for as long as you remember. It's the only existence you know. The Lord asks, "Do you want to be made well?"

Maybe you are surrounded by other Christians, by entire churches, by clergy and denominational officials who only know dependency. You feel strongly the peer pressure to maintain the status quo, to try to keep the tap of foreign money open and flowing. "Do you want to be made well?"

Maybe we are afraid that we will lose members, lose churches, lose clergy – and in fact, that may happen. But if those people refuse to believe the gospel and grow in Christ, thereby hindering other people from growing in Christ, are they really concerned about Christ or his agenda for his church? To be held back by fear of losing members may show our unwillingness to be Christ's steward and disciple.

Christ calls us to move forward with him, not in reverse away from him. Dependency is a sickness, a paralysis that Christ can heal. But we must want him to do so. The only way to escape this dependency on somebody else's money is for us Christians to learn how to be the stewards God has called us to be.

CHAPTER THREE

Dead End Number Two

I was walking around town just before sunset on the main street in the Kenyan city of Nakuru. I noticed someone following me – a slender man in a white shirt, dark trousers, and sandals. I greeted him and learned his name was David.

"What brings you out on the street just as the day is ending, David?"

"I sell maps," he said, showing me what was in his bag, the kind of maps one might see in a school classroom. I had no need for such an item, but I chose to continue talking with him. Eventually I got around to asking whether he was a Christian.

"Yes," he replied. We began talking about the church he attended. I learned that his church emphasized God's power to help with human problems and needs (true enough) – but also that if people just have enough faith, God will do miracles in their lives and they will never be poor again.

I became curious. "Do they tell you that in order to demonstrate your faith, you have to put money in the offering?" I asked. "Is it the teaching that you have to plant a seed that will grow into the miracle God will do?"

"Yes," he said.

Now the discussion was wide open to talk about the place of money in the Christian life. We explored the wealth of his pastor "He's very rich," David said – and how the man might have gotten that way. I turned the conversation to what the Word of God teaches.

"Do you read the Bible, David?" I asked.

He said, "Yes, I have a Bible right here with me."

"That is good," I replied. "There we find that being a Christian is not about getting rich or having God work miracles; it's about knowing and following Jesus as our Lord. It's about loving God more and more with all our heart and loving our neighbour as ourselves."

It was at this point that David pulled a small card out of his wallet to show me. "I'm in trouble," he confessed. "They gave these cards to everyone at church last Sunday, and we are all supposed to bring 200 shillings to the offering this coming Sunday. They promised God would answer a special prayer if we did."

"I'm just a peddler," he continued with a serious face. "I am a poor man. I don't make enough from these maps to even take care of my family. Can you help me so I have something to give on Sunday?"

At this point, I got upset, not with David but with the leaders of his church. "Do you mean that these leaders are demanding that you bring money that you don't have so that they can spend it on themselves? Can you see how these people find many ways to steal from you, but they won't lift a finger to help you learn how to become a follower of Jesus?" Whoever they were, they were not behaving like people who know and love Jesus.

But I didn't want to leave him completely disappointed. "Can I have a look at your maps?" I asked.

He showed me the two he had. "I'll take that one." I am now the proud owner of a map of Kenya. Meanwhile, David went home with a lot to think and pray about.

A Different Message

Most African villages and towns and cities are full of churches of every kind, many proclaiming salvation from sin and its effects through trusting in Christ. But the prosperity gospel is aiming for something very different. The core of the movement is this: If you have real, positive faith and you declare your faith by saying, for example, "God is making me prosperous", "God is making me well", "I am healed", or "I am rich", then God is obligated to respond to your faith and give you the blessings you are claiming. As you demonstrate your faith by sacrificial giving, he will make you wealthy and healthy beyond anything you could imagine.

There are variations of this, of course. But the whole goal of this kind of Christianity is to secure God's blessings. If those blessings are not yours yet, these people teach that it must be because you don't have the necessary faith.[2]

Making the Bible Say What It Doesn't Say

Where did this teaching come from? It came out of what began as a genuine movement of God. From the 1960s within mainline Protestant and even Roman Catholic churches, there was a spectrum of openness to Pentecostal experiences such as speaking in tongues, prophecy, healing, and even exorcism. The Presbyterian church where I came to faith experienced charismatic renewal in the early 1970s. Accompanying the tongues-speaking, prophecies, and expressive worship in my home church were several dramatic healings, including a little girl who was miraculously healed of a rare form of bone cancer in her skull. Ever since I experienced the work of the Holy Spirit as a teenager in this congregation, I have viewed myself as a charismatic Christian.

The Pentecostal and Charismatic movement emphasized the whole range of spiritual gifts God wanted to give to his people (not just speaking in tongues) and the good things God wanted to do for and through his people as we used his gifts. God remained sovereign in the process. He gave and did as he saw fit and for his own glory.

The prosperity gospel and the "Word of Faith" movement both emerged from the genuine revival of the Pentecostal movement, but they have changed into something that no longer resembles the gospel.[3] In the prosperity gospel, God becomes a means to my own happiness. The "Word of Faith" movement teaches that by declaring something with enough faith, believers can create their own realities.

> In the prosperity gospel, God becomes a means to my own happiness.

These teachers shift the focus away from God and misinterpret God's Word to say what they believe their followers want to hear. For example, a frequently quoted verse, especially when a preacher is getting ready to take an offering, is Luke 6:38: "Give, and it will be given to you. A good measure, pressed down, shaken together, running over, will be put into your lap; for the measure you give will be the measure you get back" (NRSV-A). These words come straight from the mouth of Jesus. But in what context? In just the previous verses, Jesus is talking about being generous with the poor, even lending them money without a guarantee of repayment. "Be merciful, just as your Father is merciful" (Luke 6:36).

Many preachers promise that Jesus died to give us wealth for ourselves, quoting 2 Corinthians 8:9, "For you know the generous act of our Lord Jesus Christ, that though he was rich, yet for your sakes he became poor, so that by his poverty you might become rich." But Kenyan pastor Kenneth Mbugua explains:

> If you read the context of 1 Corinthians 8, you soon discover that it is about Christians giving to others. Furthermore, the

Christians that Paul was asking the Corinthians to emulate in their sacrificial giving were themselves very poor . . . *"their abundant joy and their extreme poverty have overflowed in a wealth of generosity on their part."* [2 Corinthians 8:2]

Paul is holding up, as an example of godliness, the poor Christians in Macedonia who still sacrificed to meet the needs of others. Then in the ninth verse of the chapter, to make his point, Paul compared them to the far greater example of the one who sacrificed himself for our good.

It is completely wrong, therefore, to read this chapter and conclude that it is about *us getting rich*. On the contrary, giving us two examples to follow, God is teaching us through the Apostle Paul that we should live sacrificially and generously . . .

[As Philippians 2:4-7 explains,] the riches that Christ (temporarily) gave up for us were heavenly and spiritual riches. And, ultimately, these are the riches that Christ died to win for us: reconciliation and communion with God (John 17:24).[4]

Health and prosperity teachers confuse their listeners about what Scripture really says. When people have faith that God will do something he actually never promised to do in his Word, they can easily be disappointed and become angry at God or blame themselves for their lack of faith.

False Faith

In the church where I experienced such good charismatic renewal and many spiritual wonders, some sick people over whom we prayed so earnestly stayed sick and even died. Some paralyzed people remained in their wheelchairs. Some blind people remained unseeing.

Of course, some people told us the problem wasn't the inability or unwillingness of God, but that our faith was insufficient. In other words, it was our fault that these people remained in their state of suffering. The new "Word of Faith" teaching hurt people who trusted God to answer their prayers by adding the pain of being blamed for their lack of faith.

Prosperity teaching can look very similar to the problem that led to the Protestant Reformation. People were being encouraged to buy forgiveness of sins for themselves and for their dead relatives so that a cathedral could be built at the church headquarters. Martin Luther and other people exposed the leaders' corruption and showed from the Bible that we cannot earn or buy forgiveness. Our own good works cannot save us – only God can. Too often "having enough faith" can become a work we must do to earn God's blessing.

How much faith is necessary to work a miracle or to be healed of stage four cancer? It is a very easy (and spiritually abusive) thing to say that people are not well or not blessed financially because they don't have enough faith. But what is enough? And it doesn't even begin to address the questions: "What if God does not choose to heal me, or bless me with a million US dollars, or give me a new fancy car?"

Of course, the biggest mistake is when people are treating "faith" as if it is a thing, something we have, a kind of commodity we can exchange or give in order to get this or that blessing. But nowhere in the New Testament is faith understood to be a thing. Rather faith is our *relationship* with God. The heart of any relationship is our ability to trust. And when it comes to God, our faith is expressed in the context of our willingness to trust God whatever our circumstances are, even when it is hard. The so-called faith teachers would use faith in such a way as to *obligate* God to do what we think he should do. The New Testament emphasizes just the opposite. Faith is meant to make *us* willing to do whatever God would have us do. Real, biblical faith says: "Your kingdom come, your will be done on earth as it is in heaven" (Matthew 6:10).

Sometimes, relying on "faith" can also become an excuse for avoiding work, which is the way God often chooses to provide for people's needs. Femi Adeleye, a long-time leader in the evangelical student movement, describes how the leaders of the Christian Union on a Nigerian campus planned an all-night prayer meeting for the night before exam week:

> Students left the meeting claiming success and believing they would be "heads" and not "tails" in the forthcoming exams on the basis of Deuteronomy 28:13.
>
> Weeks after the final examination, many of them were shocked to find they had failed ... Many had been too busy with various CU meetings and outreaches to attend to their studies. Several had skipped lectures because they were too tired from long late-night meetings ... They had not studied enough, yet they expected God to reward them with good grades because of their faith.[5]

The Fertile Soils of African Hearts

The prosperity gospel and the "Word of Faith" teaching that undergirds it did not originate in Africa. My home country, America, must accept most of the responsibility.

However, the seeds of this teaching have found fertile soil to grow across the continent of Africa. The prosperity gospel resonates with aspects of many African Traditional Religions. There are, of course, thousands of variations of religious practices under the umbrella of African Traditional Religions, so one must be careful not to treat them as if they are all the same. But they have certain assumptions and perspectives in common.

Before the advent of mission Christianity, everything in most African cultures was seen in religious terms. One main purpose of religious practices was to avoid curses and to secure blessings instead. The curses to avoid were sickness, early death, a barren womb, accidents, losses to one's flocks or herds, drought, or pests afflicting one's crops. Blessings included fruitful wombs and safe deliveries, healthy children, plentiful rain, bountiful harvests, growing flocks and herds, recovery from sickness, and respected standing in the community. The causes and solutions to these challenges were seen as religious. So people consulted the resident diviner, sacrificed, or performed rituals to appease the spirits and ancestors or to undo the evil words caused by a human agent.

> The prosperity gospel has successfully tapped into this deep cultural fear of being cursed and this profound desire for blessing that is measured by one's success and health.

Prosperity preachers often quote the Old Testament, where God is viewed as the fountain of prosperity and blessing. The description of blessing on crops, animals, and wombs resonates with the traditional African vision of prosperity. The prosperity gospel has successfully tapped into this deep cultural fear of being cursed and this profound desire for blessing that is measured by one's success and health. By twisting the gospel teaching on faith, these teachers make it seem that God's main purpose is to bless us (as we understand blessing) and that we access this blessing through our faith. In today's economy this blessing is increasingly understood in terms of money rather than in terms of flocks and herds.

These preachers have changed Christianity from a religion of reconciled relationships into a religion of "this for that" (*quid pro quo*). In other words, for a certain amount of faith (and money contributed to the leader) God will give you what you need or want. We are looking for a formula with simple steps, like those that diviners give, a ritual to perform to solve our problems in the spiritual realm. But it reduces our relationship with God to transactions, as if he is a shopkeeper or an errand boy there to meet our needs. It's true that God listens to the prayers of his people and he cares for their needs, but he is also sovereign. We cannot force him to do anything he doesn't plan to do, no matter how much faith we have.

When we treat faith or obedience as if it is a currency to get blessings, we treat the covenant as if it is merely a contract: "Do these things and you're fine. Don't do these things and you're in trouble." But a covenant primarily defines a relationship. In the Old Testament, Israel constantly broke the covenant and experienced the curses. But the curses themselves were not the problem. The consequences to not keeping a covenant were a symptom that something was wrong with the relationship. These consequences revealed they were straying outside the boundaries of the love God intended for his people. Too often we focus on the surface level, asking "What can I get away with?" instead of, "How can I love God and love my neighbour?" We cannot restore our relationship with God through our own obedience, and we have all failed to love God and others. That is why Jesus had to come and die for us, taking the curse in our place. Jesus is the only way to reconciled relationships and eternal blessing.

Unfortunately, people keep misinterpreting Scripture to suggest other ways to achieve blessing through our actions. It has become popular to urge people to demonstrate to God that they have faith by contributing so-called seed money in the offering, expecting that such faith will result in a return on their investment. It should surprise no one that the ones who benefit from this arrangement are the pastors, bishops, prophets, and apostles who proclaim such faith as the way to prosperity. These leaders declare themselves to be living examples of what faith can do. They are the men and women of God whom God has blessed and anointed, or so they claim. In reality, ministry has become a lucrative business for them, and they have become professionals at persuading people to release their hard-earned money into the preachers' pockets.

These leaders prey on their members' hope for a better life, often making their members even poorer. As Femi Adeleye says:

> The prosperity gospel no longer brings good news to the poor. Some women skip going to church because they do not feel they have the right clothes or have nothing to put into any of the multiple collections. Many who do go to church expecting their personal miracle feel a sense of abandonment. As they see others dancing to the front, they feel a sense of diminished self-worth, even though they know that some of those who dance to the front only go through the motions without putting anything into the offering basket. Outside church, the pains of poverty give them a diminished sense of dignity as they struggle to make ends meet.[6]

The prosperity gospel is seriously mistaken on many levels, but the primary problem is that it subverts both stewardship and discipleship. Christianity is a Christ-centred religion that's about loving God and neighbour with all I am and have. The prosperity gospel changes it into a religion that is fundamentally me-centred and concerned about avoiding curse and securing blessing. Jesus is celebrated by the prosperity preachers for being the gateway to blessing and the source of healing. But they don't tell the story of Jesus as the *Lord* who we obey and serve.

Stewardship is forgotten. Instead, offerings are intended to leverage greater blessing (read: more stuff and more money) from God. In the hands of these so-called men and women of God, Christianity has become a get-rich-quick scam. But the only ones who are getting rich are the preachers themselves.

This is not a new phenomenon. The apostle Paul warned Timothy: "For the time is coming when people will not put up with sound doctrine, but having itching ears, they will accumulate for themselves teachers to suit their own desires" (2 Timothy 4:3). The highway is broad that leads away from Christ, away from following him as a disciple, from living as his steward.

Prosperity Everywhere!

A friend of mine assisted the leadership of a large Anglican church. The assigned preacher for the day was not known for his skill in the pulpit. As the preacher began his message in his usual fashion, my friend pulled out his smart phone to check his email and read the news. But things the preacher was saying and the way he was saying them caught his attention. This was not the preacher's usual style or content. He sounded like the health and prosperity preachers one might hear on television.

My friend picked up on a phrase that the preacher kept repeating and searched for it online. To his surprise, his search took him straight to an American televangelist's sermon. The local preacher had copied this televangelist's entire sermon word-for-word and was now feeding undiluted health and prosperity teaching to the congregation. If this is happening even in old mission churches such as the Anglican Church, it is also likely happening across the denominational spectrum all across the continent.

I once preached about the health and prosperity gospel at our university chapel service where I teach. I quoted from a news article describing the unbelievable wealth of Nigerian prosperity preachers, who were now buying jets to get them to their meetings from one end of the country to another.

One of the preachers justified such extravagant wealth and spending while living in such a poor country by saying that God had blessed him with the money to buy this jet and everything else he had, and that God would give him even more, and he would use it to buy even bigger jets. I had intended for the climax of this example to leave my audience just as appalled as I was at the corruption of Christianity.

But instead, the hall full of students cheered the defence this man gave for his jet! They even stood and whooped when I read the portion where he said that God had blessed him and that God would give him even more. My point was not getting across at all.

Like my students, the people who hear this preaching and take part in the altar calls often don't know any better. They think this is Christianity, and that meeting my needs is what the Christian God is all about.

But as we have seen, the health and prosperity gospel takes a few things that can be found in Christianity – such as healing, answered prayer, and provision for God's people – and makes them the centre of spiritual focus and Christian experience. Prosperity preachers isolate a good thing in the Scriptures, but they make it the most important thing. Overdoing one thing – whether healing or provision or miracles – has led to undoing everything else. The resulting gospel is not the gospel at all, but a formula to try to get what we want from God.

Invasive Species

One of my running routes takes me along the shores of Lake Victoria. As I looked across the lake today, a mat of green water hyacinth covered the lake, as far as the eye could see. This plant is native to South America, and it was probably introduced into Lake Victoria via the Kagera River flowing from Rwanda in the 1980s. Maybe someone who liked its blue-purple flowers used it as an exotic addition to their ornamental pond.

But once it got established in Lake Victoria, nothing could stop it from growing and spreading. It has no natural enemies, and the temperature and conditions in the lake are agreeable. Now it covers vast areas along the shoreline, and spreads when pieces of the floating mat break off and are driven by winds to distant shores. It disrupts local fishing and industry and interferes with water systems. Worst of all, it enhances breeding grounds for mosquitoes carrying malaria and water snails carrying bilharzia.

The health and prosperity heresy is also an invasive species to the African continent. It has found conditions on the ground agreeable and is rapidly spreading from coast to coast. Because too few people are theologically trained, the preachers propagating their message operate with impunity. Because many preachers operate independent ministries, they are accountable to no one. Very few people are getting very rich off the offerings of desperate people. The world is looking at some Christian leaders and wondering whether they are any different from corrupt leaders in business and politics.

> The health and prosperity heresy is also an invasive species to the African continent. It has found conditions on the ground agreeable and is rapidly spreading from coast to coast.

To weed out the false teaching destroying the faith from within, we need an understanding of biblical stewardship. African Christians certainly don't need me to sound the alarm. Many are already writing on this subject, such as Femi Adeleye, John Musyimi, Kenneth Mbugua, Conrad Mbewe, Michael Otieno Maura, and others. They are studying the Bible, theology, and history and using their insights to teach others how serious the problem of the health and prosperity heresy has become. Let's follow their example and pray for more African Christians to become stewards of the gospel and disciples of our self-sacrificing Lord.

PART TWO
Wisdom Not to Be Forgotten

CHAPTER FOUR

Should Christians Tithe like in the Old Testament?

We have discussed how dependency and prosperity are two dangerous misunderstandings of what the Bible teaches about faith. In the next four chapters, we will study what the Bible says and what the early church practised when it came to money, stewardship, and giving. We'll begin here with a look at tithing, another way many Christians are told to manage their money, which comes from the Old Testament. It is appealing because it seems so simple and so *biblical*. But is tithing the answer, especially when we look more closely at what the Scriptures actually say?

Churches all over the world encourage their members to tithe. For pastors and elder boards, tithing is an easy concept to grasp and communicate. Could it be any clearer than an obligation to give "10 per cent for the Lord"? No doubt the concept is easier for you and me to understand than to practise, if the money we make barely covers rent, food, school fees, transport, and helping with extended family needs.

But then, like most African Christians, we also have many preachers' favourite tithing passage ringing in our ears:

Will anyone rob God? Yet you are robbing me! But you say, 'How are we robbing you?' In your tithes and offerings! You are cursed with a curse, for you are robbing me – the whole nation of you! Bring the full tithe into the storehouse, so that there may be food in my house, and thus put me to the test, says the Lord of hosts; see if I will not open the windows of heaven for you and pour down for you an overflowing blessing (Malachi 3:8-10 NRSV-A).

When you hear this reminder from your church leaders perhaps you feel guilty. You do not want to disappoint God, much less call down a curse on your head and on your nation! So maybe you give whenever you hear this message, but you still struggle to manage 10 per cent consistently.

On the other hand, perhaps this Scripture excites you with hope. You imagine that all your other money problems will be solved by the promise that God will pour down his overflowing blessing! Maybe you give in faith, trusting that God will provide for your needs. Perhaps you or someone around you has a testimony of how God has provided for you because you decided to trust him and tithe.

If you are a church leader, you may be struggling with the church's finances. The costs of the church building, a sound system, keyboard, and paying staff are all a challenge. Visitors need to be hosted, the needy in the community or the church assisted, and the children taught about God. All of these require resources. Yet there is very little money coming in.

Perhaps the church leadership expects the pastor to work full time at church but there is not enough offering for both the needs of the church and the pastor's family. So the pastor or the pastor's spouse must find another way of supplementing the family income.

In situations like this, tithing seems like an easy solution. If all the people in the church gave 10 per cent, the result would be that as soon as there were 10 employed people in the church the pastor would have the average of their income each month. Of course, there should be more church members than that, so that the church's needs would be sorted out and the church would have extra funds for ministering to the community, going on mission trips, and building better facilities.

What Does the Bible Actually Say?

The financial needs of the church in Africa and its members are real. But as we look at the actual biblical evidence, we discover that the Old Testament concept of tithing may not be the answer for New Testament stewards like us. So where does the idea of tithing come from?

It comes from verses found throughout the Old Testament, in the law God gave the people of Israel. Before we treat the Old Testament as if it directly applies to us today, we need to ask why it was written and for what purpose.

> A principle of good Bible interpretation is that we must understand the books of the Bible as they were originally intended before we apply them to our lives.

We should not treat this ancient collection of stories, poems, histories, and prophecies as God's direct word for whatever situation we face. I am not saying that the Old Testament is irrelevant to us today. It certainly has God-given value. We just need to maintain the big picture.

The various books that make up the Old Testament were written to the nation of Israel. A principle of good Bible interpretation is that we must understand them as they were originally intended before we apply them to our lives. To unlock the unified message of the Old Testament in general, and commands like tithing in particular, we must understand that the commands were given in the context of a specific agreement that God made with Israel, also called a *covenant* (Exodus 19–24). Once we grasp what God is doing with his covenant with Israel, we will understand the Old Testament as we never have before.

God's Covenant with Israel[7]

In ancient Near Eastern history, a covenant was an agreement made between two parties – often between a greater king and a lesser, conquered people. The king usually identified himself on the basis of the great feats he had accomplished, and for his part, agreed to protect the newly conquered people and provide necessary services. The people agreed to keep the king's laws, pay taxes, and provide a certain number of young men, horses, and supplies for his army. Then the gods would be called to bless the people for keeping the covenant or curse them if they broke it and rebelled against their lord. There would usually be a long list of terrible things that the king would threaten to do to the people should they throw off the yoke of his reign over them. These are the types of covenants that were common among Israel's neighbours in the time of Genesis and Exodus.

The covenant we find in Exodus, Leviticus, Numbers, and Deuteronomy is similar to this. The great king *Yahweh* (God's Hebrew name is unpronounceable, so it is always translated in English as the Lord or LORD) identified himself as the one who saved Israel from Egypt with mighty acts of power. He called Israel to be his people and promised that he would be their God. "I am the Lord your God, who brought you out of the land of Egypt, out of the house of slavery" (Exodus 20:2). Then he outlined the conditions of the covenant – the laws about how his people will relate to him and to one another. These were summarized in the Ten Commandments (Exodus 20:3-17) and expanded through the rest of the *Torah* (the name in Hebrew given to the first five books of the Hebrew Scriptures).

God's covenantal commands covered almost every aspect of Israel's life and worship. Not only were there commands about what sacrifices to bring, when to bring them, and how to offer them, but there were commands about the various festivals to be held every year. God commanded the Israelites to refrain from working every seventh day (the Sabbath). He commanded them to eat only certain kinds of animals and not others. He commanded ritual purification after contact with a dead body or sexual relations – emissions (for men) and menstruation (for women). God commanded mothers to be purified after childbirth and baby boys to be circumcised. Also as part of God's covenant commandments, God required each family to bring their tithes and offerings to the Lord. These were all part of the covenant that God made with Israel at Mount Sinai.

Along with the covenant's obligations, God also promised benefits or blessings for faithfulness and obedience. There were also stern warnings about what would happen if the people chose to rebel and follow other gods or if they did not keep God's commandments.

Covenants like this one would then be ratified with all the people participating in solemn sacrifices. They would agree to fulfil all that the king required of them, and the king would agree to do all that he had promised to do for them.

Israel Failed to Keep the Covenant[8]

Tragically, Israel chose again and again to rebel against Yahweh. They broke the covenant, calling down on their heads the curses God declared would happen if his people ever left him for other gods or otherwise broke the relationship between them. The historical books of the Old Testament tell how again and again the people went their own way, experienced terrible judgement, and then came back to the Lord in repentance.

God was extremely longsuffering; he did not give up on his people. He sent a new type of character, the prophet, who called the people of Israel to account and warned them of God's coming judgement if they did not repent. Let me point out that the prophets of the Bible do not exactly match our cultural understanding of prophets. Many African cultures see a prophet as a holy man who can foretell the future, who mediates between factions in the community, and who presides at sacrifices or other religious functions. Old Testament prophets such as Samuel, for example, sometimes filled these roles in the community. But the main reason God raised up prophets was to remind his people of the covenant they had solemnly made with him and to warn them of being cursed by the threatened judgement if they persisted in their rebellion.

We might say that Old Testament prophets were God's lawyers, making a case against God's people who had broken their covenant agreement and the law. Their writings are full of both the threats of judgement for having left their God, and also the promise of God's blessing if they repent and come back "home". To give a clear example, listen again to the words of the prophet Malachi quoted earlier:

> Will anyone rob God? Yet you are robbing me! But you say, 'How are we robbing you?' In your tithes and offerings! You are cursed with a curse, for you are robbing me – the whole nation of you! Bring the full tithe into the storehouse, so that there may be food in my house, and thus put me to the test, says the Lord of hosts; see if I will not open the windows of heaven for you and pour down for you an overflowing blessing (Malachi 3:8-10).

Now that we know the story of the Old Testament, the covenant, and the role of a prophet, this Scripture makes more sense. Malachi was reminding Israel that they had made a covenant with the Lord, promising to tithe. They would be cursed if they broke the covenant, and abundantly blessed if they were faithful to the covenant. All of these curses and blessings were based on the fact that Israel and the Lord had made a covenant long before, in the time of Moses.

Unfortunately, even after all the prophets' warnings, Israel still failed to keep God's covenant. So God brought about the judgement he had promised. The 10 northern tribes of Israel were defeated and scattered all over the Middle East by the Assyrians. Not long afterwards, the kingdom of Judah was crushed by the Babylonians. Jerusalem was destroyed, the Temple was burned, and the survivors were taken in captivity to Babylon. And even after the exiles returned, they still struggled to take God's covenant seriously. This is the context of Malachi's prophecy – a warning to take their covenantal relationship with God seriously, or even worse things would befall them. Judea continued on, but mostly as a small province constantly pressured by the surrounding peoples to abandon their covenant and conform to their neighbours' ways of living. Except for a brief period before the Romans, they never fully recovered as a people, but lived under constant threat of annihilation by their more powerful neighbours. The New Testament begins with the Jewish people suffering under Roman rule, hoping that God will come to their aid and deliver them from their enemies.

Tithing in the Old Covenant

As we have seen, tithing was one of the conditions, or commandments, that God gave to Israel as part of his covenant with them. The purpose for these tithes was to support Israel's worship as well as provide for the poor. But there has been a lot of confusion, not just about who is obligated to pay these tithes, but even how much a tithe was in Israel's day.

Most of our churches teach that the Old Testament tithe is 10 per cent of one's income, so we should give 10 per cent to our churches. Some churches even make giving 10 per cent a requirement for membership. But is this 10 per cent figure what we find in God's law? It will likely come as a shock, but nowhere does the Old Testament teach or require that members of the Sinai covenant community are meant to give only 10 per cent. I believe when we study the laws of the Old Testament, we see that the required figure is actually significantly *more*.

> The Old Testament tithe *is not 10 per cent, it's actually 23.3 per cent of one's income every year.*

Here's how Moses put it in Deuteronomy 12:5-19, 14:22-26, and 26:1-15. Every head of household was required to give 10 per cent for the support and upkeep of the Tabernacle/Temple and to provide for the Levites, who had no land inheritance. Then, every head of household was required to contribute a *second* 10 per cent of their income, intended to cover expenses when the family travelled to Jerusalem for the major festivals every year. Finally, a *third* 10 per cent was to be collected every three years (for an average of 3.3 per cent per year) for the widows, orphans, and refugees in one's local area.

Does it surprise you to learn that the Old Testament tithe *is not 10 per cent, it's actually 23.3 per cent of one's income every year?*

The modern concept of tithing just 10 per cent to the church, which is so prevalent in many of our churches, is thus actually less than the Old Testament concept. That commandment to tithe was given in the context of the covenant God made with his people Israel at Mount Sinai – the same as circumcision, keeping the Sabbath, and kosher eating restrictions. This system was intended for the nation of Israel, not for any of Israel's neighbouring people.[9]

What about Us?[10]

How are we Christians supposed to interpret and apply the Old Testament? Beyond tithing, how do we apply its many other commands about sacrificing, eating kosher, keeping Sabbath, and circumcising baby boys? It was written for the children of Israel, but what does it mean for the rest of us who are not Jews?

Christians have struggled with this from the earliest days of the church until now. In fact, Acts records a massive conflict on this very issue. Plenty of Christians in Jerusalem were convinced that Christianity was essentially an add-on component to their Judaism. When Gentiles began becoming Christians through the ministries of Peter, Philip, Paul, and Barnabas, many Jewish Christians were scandalized. They struggled to believe that non-Jews could become Christians. So, they insisted that all Christians, both Jews and Gentiles, keep the Old Testament covenant. This meant that a Gentile man would have to get circumcised in order to be a real Christian, as well as eat kosher, keep the Sabbath, and follow all the other Old Testament laws.

This understanding of Christianity was very different from the one the apostles had been preaching. The issue was so serious that Paul and other apostles in Jerusalem felt that the gospel itself was being threatened. The church's leadership needed to decide how Christians would relate to the Jewish Scriptures and its covenant commands. They had to discern: Is the Jesus movement just a sect within Judaism, or is Jesus doing something bigger, something more universal?

It was so important to get this right that they called a special conference of leaders in Jerusalem (see Acts 15). James, the overseer or bishop of the Jerusalem church, presided. They heard from all of the people involved. They heard the opinion of Jewish Christians. They heard from the apostles Paul and Barnabas, who argued that even Jews couldn't fully keep the Jewish covenant, so Jesus had come both to save Jews from the curse of their failure and to make a way for Gentiles to be saved apart from the Jewish law. It was a complicated argument, but for the sake of the gospel they worked through it. They came to a resolution that saved the church from division and saved the gospel from being obliterated.

These first Christians made a very important decision that day. It had implications for the subsequent history of the church right up to our present day. They decided that *Christianity was not Judaism.* In other words, the Jewish Scriptures were not written directly for Christians in the same way they were for Jews. God did not make his covenant at Mount Sinai with Gentiles or with Christians; he made his covenant with Jews. The prophets were usually not addressing Gentiles, much less Christians; they were calling Jews to repent for breaking their covenant with God. So, the rules, regulations, and obligations we find in the Old Testament were intended for the Jews and Jews alone – not for Gentiles.[11]

Paul, Peter, James, and the first Christians understood that the primary blessing from the Hebrew Scriptures is that we learn about God and his ways, and of his promises to send a Saviour. The Sinai covenant did not apply to Gentiles, but the Jewish Scriptures still revealed many relevant things about the power, character, and plans of God. The Scriptures also pointed to a future salvation that God would accomplish when he sent a Saviour. The Messiah would deliver his people from their rebellion against God and the curses that such rebellion brought upon their lives and their nation. These same Scriptures also explained that God was not finished with the many nations across the world. His Messiah would open the way for his blessing to come to them as well.

When Jesus came as the Messiah, he did what Israel never could; he kept both the letter and the spirit of God's law. Israel, just like the rest of humanity, had rebelled against God, become alienated from God, and become lost to sin and death. Jesus saves Israel from the covenant curses that destroyed Israel when they left the way of the

Torah, and Jesus saves us from the curses of our own estrangement from God and from our resulting death by taking the consequences of our fall upon himself. His death on the cross ratified a *new* covenant open to all people, which we celebrate in the Eucharist. This new covenant would be about repentance, relationship, and forgiveness, not the commandments, condemnation, and curses of the old.

Jesus defeated the power of sin and death and rose again from the dead. He is the beginning of God's new creation and new humanity. By the power of the Holy Spirit, when we resurrect from the dead on the Last Day, we will become part of that new humanity. As Jeremiah prophesied: "This is the covenant that I will make with the house of Israel after those days, says the Lord: I will put my law within them, and I will write it on their hearts; and I will be their God, and they shall be my people" (Jeremiah 31:33). Ezekiel declares: "A new heart I will give you, and a new spirit I will put within you; and I will remove from your body the heart of stone and give you a heart of flesh" (Ezekiel 36:26).

Because of Jesus, *all* nations are invited to become part of the New Covenant community, whose mission is to establish New Covenant communities of Jesus-followers to the ends of the earth.

The Big Issue for Paul

Even after the Jerusalem Council's decision, some early Christians assumed that they were still obligated to keep the Old Testament commands. Like many of us today, they had a very difficult time understanding the new regimen for followers of Jesus. But Paul insisted that as Christians under the New Covenant, it is crucial that we do not put ourselves back under the Jewish Torah.

Paul makes this point forcefully in his letter to the churches in Galatia. He was upset to discover that Jewish Christians had been following him from town to town during his recent mission there, seeking to persuade the Galatian Christians to abandon Paul's gospel. These troublemakers taught that for people's Christianity to be viable they must embrace and keep the Jewish covenant in order to become true members of God's special people.

Paul was furious. You can still feel the heat of his anger when he writes: "I am astonished that you are so quickly deserting the one who called you in the grace of Christ and are turning to a different gospel – not that there is another gospel, but there are some that are confusing you and want to pervert the gospel of Christ" (Galatians 1:6-7). Notice that for Paul, this is not a matter of different interpretations; the gospel itself is in danger. The threat introduced by these false teachers is so real that Paul declares: "But even if we or an angel from heaven should proclaim to you a gospel contrary to what we proclaimed to you, let that one be accursed!" (Galatians 1:8). These are very strong words.

> This is not a matter of different interpretations; the gospel itself is in danger.

Paul was so convicted that it was wrong to go back to living under the Torah that at one point he directly confronted Peter about this very issue. In another part of his letter to the Galatians, he describes how Peter struggled to be consistent in his understanding about the gospel and whether Christians should continue to live like Jews under the Old Covenant or not. So, we are not alone in finding it difficult to separate ourselves from the Old Testament law.

In Antioch, which had been Paul and Barnabas's home base for their missionary journeys, Jewish and Gentile Christians mixed freely and had fellowship together. This was against Jewish law, which said Jews could not associate with or eat with Gentiles. During a visit, Peter had been freely eating with all the Christians in Antioch. But when he heard that some of the Jewish Christians that demanded Gentile circumcision were arriving from Jerusalem, he separated himself from the Gentile believers and stayed with the Jewish believers. Paul felt that this was more than just hypocrisy: "'If you, though a Jew, live like a Gentile and not like a Jew, how can you compel the Gentiles to live like Jews?' We ourselves are Jews by birth and not Gentile sinners; yet we know that a person is justified not by the works of the law but through faith in Jesus Christ" (Galatians 2:14b-16a).

I need to add here an important point that is not clear in the English rendering. In Galatians, every time the apostle Paul uses the word translated into English as "law", he is using the Greek translation of the Hebrew word *Torah*. This word means "instruction", but it also stands for the first five books of the Hebrew Scriptures and thus for the Sinai covenant contained therein. The issue for Paul is not keeping generic laws or doing good works to be saved. Rather, Paul is saying something that would be shocking for a Jew to say: Jews are not saved by keeping *Torah*, and by their resulting identity as Jews. "We we have come to believe in Christ Jesus, so that we might be justified by faith in Christ, and not by doing the works of the law [*Torah*] because no one will be justified by the works of the law [*Torah*]" (Galatians 2:16). These "works of the law [*Torah*]" are none other than those things which set Jews apart from the rest of the Gentile world, which included circumcision, eating kosher, keeping the Sabbath, and tithing.

Paul is clearly vexed:

> You foolish Galatians! Who has bewitched you? . . . The only thing I want to learn from you is this: Did you receive the Spirit by doing the works of the law [*Torah*] or by believing what you heard? Are you so foolish? Having started with the Spirit, are you now ending with the flesh? (Galatians 3:1-3).

Then Paul cuts to the heart of his issue with the Galatians. He says we are not justified by following the *Torah* as Christians, for the simple reason that:

> All who rely on the works of the law [*Torah*] are under a curse; for it is written, 'Cursed is everyone who does not observe and obey all the things written in the book of the law [*Torah*].' Now it is evident that no one is justified before God by the law [*Torah*]; for 'The one who is righteous will live by faith.' . . . Christ redeemed us from the curse of the law [*Torah*] by becoming a curse for us – for it is written, 'Cursed is everyone who hangs on a tree' – in order that in Christ Jesus the blessing of Abraham might come to the Gentiles, so that we might receive the promise of the Spirit through faith (Galatians 3:10-14).

The implications of Paul's argument are clear and startling. When we Christians force ourselves and others to keep the Old Testament laws, we try to do something that even the Jews couldn't do. Paul's point is that the Jews have reaped again and again the curses that come upon those who cannot and will not keep the stipulations of the Sinai covenant. He cannot imagine that anyone would be so insane as to want to go back into an arrangement that leads only to destruction. Paul could not be more adamant:

> Listen! I, Paul, am telling you that if you let yourselves be circumcised, Christ will be of no benefit to you. Once again, I testify to every man who lets himself be circumcised that he is obliged to obey the entire law [*Torah*]. You who want to be justified by the law [*Torah*] have cut yourselves off from Christ; you have fallen away from grace (Galatians 5:2-4).

Paul is trying with all of his considerable intellectual, rhetorical, and biblical abilities to turn the Galatians back to Christ. Because for Paul, theology matters. The teaching one receives is almost never neutral – it either leads one closer to Christ or further away from Christ. By insisting that the Galatian Christians be circumcised in order to come into line with the Jewish covenant, these teachers are marching these young Christians straight back into the condemnation of the law that Jesus had just saved them from!

Did the Early Church Practise Tithing?

But let's follow the evidence one step further. Almost all of the earliest Christians were Jews. So even if the new Gentile Christians were not required to follow the law, were these Jewish Christians meant to give a 23.3 per cent tithe just as Jews did under the covenant made at Sinai?

The examples of Christians in action in the book of Acts seem to indicate that they actually gave quite a lot more than even a Jewish tithe! These first Christians don't seem very interested in percentages. It may surprise you to know that the word *tithe(s)* appears 28 times across the Old Testament, but it appears only a few times in the entire New Testament, usually referring to Jews still trying to observe the *Torah*. Tithing is never commanded for New Testament believers.[12]

These early believers took Jesus's radical teachings on stewardship seriously. It is interesting that the amount Christians should give is not addressed in any of the literature that survives from the first century and a half of Christianity. This suggests that whatever Christians were doing, there was no controversy about it. They were simply following the practice handed down from Jesus and the apostles. Nowhere do we see any Christian leader, from the apostles themselves to their successors, the bishops, teaching that Christians must continue to practise tithing in the same way as under the Old Covenant.

The first clear record we have of what the early church taught about Old Testament tithing comes from the second century. Irenaeus, the Bishop of Lyon (in what today is southern France), wrote down what seems to be the standard procedure of Christian churches in both the West and the East. Like the examples we see in Acts, Irenaeus believed Christians were called to be stewards, not to tithe. We might expect that the early church's view of stewardship was too impractical and would fade away after the first generation. Instead, we find succeeding generations of Christians with the same motivation and practice when it comes to their wealth and possessions. Instead of a moderated view of Christian giving, Irenaeus astonishes us by matter-of-factly explaining a radical understanding of stewardship (emphasis mine):

> Therefore the offering of the church, which the Lord directed to be offered in the whole world, is accounted a pure sacrifice with God, and is acceptable to him, not that he needs a sacrifice from us, but because he who offers is himself honoured in his offering if his gift be accepted. By his offering, both honour and affection are shown to the King. And our Lord taught us to offer this in all simplicity and innocence (Matthew 5:23, 24). Therefore, we must offer to God the first fruits of his creation, as Moses said. Offerings are no longer offered by bondsmen, but by free men ... They [OT saints] offered their tithes; *but those who have received liberty set apart everything they have for the Lord's use,* cheerfully and freely giving them (2 Corinthians 9:7), not as small things in the hope of greater, but like that poor widow, who put her whole livelihood into the treasury of God (Luke 21:4).[13]

Irenaeus acknowledges the requirement to tithe under the Old Covenant, but he also asserts that the New Covenant community is under no such obligation. Instead, love carries no limit – Christians will share everything they have with those in need. Whether or not there were Christians who carried on the old practice of tithing, Irenaeus says Christians were operating under a new concept of stewardship and living under a new regime of generosity. As we shall see in the next chapter, Christ calls us to put everything we have at God's disposal.

> Christians were operating under a new concept of stewardship and living under a new regime of generosity.

Tithing was part of God's covenant with Israel on Mount Sinai. But nobody was able to keep that covenant. That is why the Messiah had to save his people and open the way of salvation for the rest of the nations as well. The Old Testament points us to the Messiah, and the New Testament introduces us to the Lord Jesus, who calls us to a new and radical life. Jesus himself is the one who introduces us to the concept of stewardship – which may amount to much more than 10 per cent!

Subsequent generations of Christians up to our own day have forgotten what the apostles taught us about the Old Testament. In spite of Paul's teaching in his letter to the Galatian Christians who were struggling with this very issue, eager Christian teachers keep trying today to impose requirements from the Old Covenant on people and churches who are instead under the New Covenant. Living as if we are under the Old Covenant erodes the church's understanding and proclamation of the gospel. As we will see in the next chapter, when we realize that everything we have is a gift from God, we will not need a law to tell us to give. Indeed, people will know we are true disciples of Christ by how we freely surrender these resources to be used for God's purposes.

CHAPTER FIVE

What Jesus Said about Money

Have you ever noticed how often Jesus talked about money? Of his 39 parables, 11 are about financial priorities and stewardship. Jesus talked more about money than he did about heaven and hell combined.

Almsgiving in the First Century

Jesus was a first-century Jew, so his teachings came in a context that is unfamiliar to many of us. Let's take a few minutes to better understand Jesus in his own setting. All good first-century Jews were expected to give to people in need. The Jewish Scriptures urge both leaders and people to "remember the poor". God promised to bless them if they were generous instead of stingy by giving or lending to the poor (Deuteronomy 15:7-8, 10-11). They were to give because giving is an aspect of who God is. He is a God who executes justice for the orphan and the widow and provides for the resident alien (Deuteronomy 10:18).

Giving to the poor or "almsgiving" is so closely tied to right relationships that in the Talmud and in the later rabbinic literature they are referred to simply as *zedakah* – righteousness[14] (via Arabic, *zedekah* metamorphosed into the Swahili word *sadaka* – offering). Perhaps surprisingly to our ears, the rabbis understood charity not so much as a kindness to the poor person but as something to which they were *entitled*, and the giver was thus *obligated* to give. As one rabbi wrote, "The poor man does more for the householder (in accepting alms) than the householder does for the poor man (by giving him the charity)", because he is giving the householder the opportunity to do something good.[15]

The idea was that everyone's things belong to God and that poverty and riches come from God. The rabbis further state in *Avot* (3:8): "Give unto him of what is his, seeing that you and what you have are his." In other words, when one gives to the poor, one is giving not what belongs to oneself but what belongs to the Lord, and thus to the poor. God blesses those who have so that they, in turn, can be God's blessing to those who have not.

Jesus's Manifesto on Money

There are many similarities between what Jesus teaches in the Gospels and what one finds in the Torah and in later rabbinic teaching about almsgiving and stewardship. In Jesus's manifesto for discipleship, the so-called Sermon on the Mount, in Matthew 5–7, he explains God's intentions underlying the Jewish law. But Jesus explains that these ancient Jewish emphases require a heart transformation. Stewardship, in Jesus's hands, becomes a lens through which one's heart comes into focus. Stewardship becomes the way we fulfil the greatest commandments, how we love God with all our heart, how we love our neighbour as ourselves.

This passage gives Christians today guidance about how to apply these Old Covenant concerns to our New Covenant lives. When it comes to giving to the poor, Jesus says "*when* you give alms." He *assumes that his followers will be giving*. His concern, instead, is that giving should be done not with an eye to impress the wider society but done secretly. People who give to win others' praise have been rewarded already, but God will reward any giving done in secret (Matthew 6:1-4).

Almost every African culture has fundraising events that provide the wealthy with a stage for flaunting both their wealth and their giving. In Kenya, *harambees* began as a cultural practice to help local communities pool together to build a school or meet a local need. Many churches now use *harambees* to raise the large sums of money that are needed for purchasing land, building structures, or other large projects. Invitations are sent to wealthy individuals and politicians. In meetings after the worship service, individuals come to the front, where their donations are announced to everyone.

> For Jesus, money is not to be an instrument of power, but of compassion.

Jesus rather bluntly questions such self-serving displays. He directs his followers to address need in ways that do not draw attention to themselves.[16] In most cultures, money and the way it is used is a main way to exercise power. For Jesus, money is not to be an instrument of power, but of compassion. Therefore, money and possessions are not to be accumulated for the sake of having more and more, or as a demonstration to everyone else of how successful or blessed a person is. Instead, if I have an abundance of wealth and a lot of stuff, God has given those resources to me for a reason. My treasure is to be used not for myself or for advancing agendas, but for good. Next, Jesus makes the uncomfortable observation that the way one uses money and "stores up treasure" is a straightforward revelation of the orientation of one's heart, because "For where your treasure is, there your heart will be also . . . No one can serve two masters; for a slave will either hate the one and love the other, or be devoted to one and despise the other. You cannot serve God and wealth" (Matthew 6:21, 24 NRSV-A).

Jesus is warning us that greed is dangerous. This reminds me of Crabtree Falls, a beautiful series of waterfalls in the United States where people hike and picnic. Signs are posted everywhere warning people not to venture into the water. But some people believe they are strong enough to avoid any danger. What could go wrong by wading in a bit? But when they get into the stream, they find a faster current and more slippery rocks than they anticipated. At least 30 people have died in the last four decades, swept over the edge of the waterfall.

Jesus's words about greed and riches are like the signs warning hikers that what seems beautiful is actually deadly. Yet we often ignore the warnings, thinking they don't apply to us. "I want to make money," we think, "as long as I do it honestly and attend church, it can't hurt." But Jesus is serious when he says we can't serve two masters. Do we trust him to know the danger?

The Rich Young Ruler

One of the most disturbing incidents in the Gospels is Jesus's conversation with a wealthy young man who wanted to know what he needed to do to gain eternal life (or "be saved"). The man said he had kept all of the commandments, so Jesus told him, "There is still one thing lacking. Sell all that you own and distribute the money to the poor, and you will have treasure in heaven; then come, follow me" (Luke 18:22).

"Surely Jesus cannot be serious," we clamour. The disciples too were astonished at how this conversation turned out. They watched the rich man walk sadly away, thinking that following Jesus cost too much. Perhaps the disciples thought to themselves: "The guy has lots of money. He would have made an excellent member of the team. He could have bankrolled your biggest projects, Jesus!"

Jesus did not help matters with his next statement: "Indeed, it is easier for a camel to go through the eye of a needle than for someone who is rich to enter the kingdom of God" (Luke 18:25). Not only does this clash with his followers' understanding of salvation, it demonstrates rather nicely that Jesus was much bigger than the box they were attempting to put him in: "Those who heard it said, 'Then who can be saved?'" (Luke 18:26).

Jesus reminded them just what an impossible reach salvation is: "He replied, 'What is impossible for mortals is possible for God'" (Luke 18:27). Salvation *is* hard; it is a narrow way, as opposed to the broad highway most would rather travel. It is hard, precisely because it touches, and intends to transform, all of our values, including the way we view and use our possessions. Repentance requires radical changes in every human heart, in putting off our old rebellion and putting on Christ and his priorities instead. It is impossible for any of us to do this on our own.

> Our desire to accumulate wealth becomes a life-threatening cancer that will destroy us if left to run its course.

This radical surgery Jesus prescribes for this wealthy young man is shocking. It's similar to the radical surgery, chemotherapy, and radiation treatment inflicted on someone who has a life-threatening cancer. Jesus knows the young man is sick, and his illness is life-threatening. So Jesus says, "Sell what you have and give the money to the poor."

More than a few Christians believe the opposite is true. Ostentatious wealth and prosperity, they say, are a sign of God's blessing. Everyone should seek more and more wealth. Lack of such "blessing" means you are missing out on what God wants to do for you. These Christians often rush to say that the rich man's wealth was not the problem.

Jesus, however, knows better. He seems to know precisely when our desire to accumulate wealth becomes a life-threatening cancer that will destroy us if left to run its course. Jesus's question to the wealthy young man was essentially: "Which is more important to you, keeping your wealth or following me?"

The young man was, like many of us, likely hoping for a third option – "Both!" But that was not offered. While the call to let go of our wealth may seem unnecessary to us, Jesus, who knows our hearts, knows the danger we are in. He knows that it's not just wealth and possessions that rust and corrode and get stolen; human hearts rust and corrode and get stolen. He knows our hearts become corrupt when wealth is accumulated and spent only on ourselves. Jesus knows that wealth tends to distract those who possess it from true life and meaning.

The Rich Young Egyptian

This story from the Gospels reminds me of an Egyptian named Anthony, who was born in the mid-third century to wealthy land-owning Christian parents. When he was 20, both his parents died. As the only son, Anthony inherited the entire estate. Shortly afterwards, in church, Anthony heard about Jesus's conversation with the rich young man. Anthony felt he was the young man Jesus was addressing. He promptly arranged for his young sister to be cared for by a group of Christian women, and then he sold his estate and gave the proceeds to help the needy and the poor.

At this point, Anthony heard Christ's call to follow him into the desert to pray. While there had been other Christian men who had fled to the desert to pursue a life of solitude, poverty, and prayer, Anthony's example spurred a movement of both men and women to take seriously Jesus's claims of discipleship in the face of the growing worldliness of the church.[17]

We know this movement today as monasticism, and God has used multitudes of these faithful men and women to preserve the church in times of peril and great darkness, as well as advancing the gospel across cultural and racial barriers. The impact of this young Egyptian's obedience is still being felt today, 1,700 years later.

More Barns, Bigger and Better!

Like any good teacher, Jesus makes his point in a variety of ways. And in doing so, he leaves no doubt as to what he is trying to say. The question is, are we willing to listen?

When someone asks Jesus to help him get his share of the inheritance from his brother, Jesus tells another story. He describes a man so rich that he built extra barns to store his harvest, expecting to relax and enjoy his wealth for years to come. But that very night, he dies. He invested everything in this life instead of investing in God's priorities. In the perspective of eternity, his stockpile of possessions was useless, and he was a fool (Luke 12:13-21).

Now, the problem with the rich man and his productive farms is not that his fields were productive or that he was making money. Rather, the rich man was greedy. He considered his earnings to be *his* to use for his own pleasure. Jesus said, "Take care! Be on your guard against all kinds of greed; for one's life does not consist in the abundance of possessions" (Luke 12:15). Often, the rich are actually impoverished when it comes to the things of God. Any of the possessions treasured by people in this life can be evidence of resources and opportunities misused.

Instead of being God's slaves who manage all the things he has given us for his glory and the love of our neighbour, we can become slaves of our money and possessions. We can become bound to our culture's expectations of how successful people should live. So, we get our degrees, climb the job ladder, earn that salary, get that car, buy that house, and take that holiday to be seen by those people. But there is always more to acquire – a better job, salary, car, house, or holiday. There is always another barn to build, until we discover that we have wasted our lives focusing on ourselves, accumulating treasure we cannot take with us when our time is up.

Jesus's story teaches that all riches are God's, and they are given by him to be used for those things he considers important. Our wealth, opportunities, education, and skills are not ours, but have been given to us by God. So, the real question is not, "How much am I giving?" but "How well am I managing the resources entrusted to me by God?"

Take a moment and reflect. Are you spending what God has given you on yourself, your pleasures, and your agenda? Or are you focused on God's priorities and God's agendas? When opportunities come your way, do you use them for your advantage, or do you consider how you could use them for God?

Trusting God to Provide

In the Sermon on the Mount, Jesus addresses one of our primary concerns, which is, "If I really trust God with everything I have, how do I know I won't run out of everything I need and just die?" Jesus responds to our deep-seated fear by talking about how we can live worry-free, like the birds in the sky and the flowers in the field (Matthew 6:25-33). Jesus's followers can be generous with what we have because we know that God – "your Father", as Jesus says – will take care of us just as he takes care of creation.

In Luke's version of the Sermon on the Mount, Jesus ends with these words: "Do not be afraid, little flock, for it is your Father's good pleasure to give you the kingdom. Sell your possessions and give alms" (Luke 12:32-33a). Being generous with our possessions is simply a matter of expressing our faith that God will take care of us, whereas worry and anxiety about possessions reveal a profound lack of trust in the God who made us and loves us.

Baptized with His Wallet

As a young man, David Kasali was very worried about having adequate possessions. His father was a poor pastor in the Democratic Republic of Congo who had struggled to provide school fees and shoes for nine children on a ministry salary.[18] David resolved to work and study hard so he wouldn't be like his father. He got a good paying job and was entrusted with the company's funds.

At the bank where David deposited the company's funds, the bank manager befriended

> "I wanted to work for my own life, to earn my own money."

him. He invited him to prayer meetings, and David realized that Christianity was a love relationship with God. At one prayer meeting, a woman told David the Lord was calling him into full-time ministry, but he had been running away. David pulled out his wallet and said:

> This is why I have been running away. I wanted to work for my own life, to earn my own money. I wanted to be able to send my children to school. It is as though, when I was baptized, I pulled my wallet out of my pocket and said, 'Don't baptize my wallet.' Today, I want my wallet to be baptized with me. I surrender it.

From that point, David's life completely changed. Now, he wanted to be like his father, totally surrendered to God in trusting dependence. David left his job and moved his family to a remote village to teach high school students and disciple them. While there, he received a scholarship to study at the Nairobi Evangelical Graduate School of Theology (NEGST, today part of Africa International University). After that, he got the opportunity to work and travel throughout Africa with the Association of Evangelicals in Africa, which left him with many questions about

Christianity in Africa. He pursued these questions in his doctoral studies in the US, then returned to teach at NEGST, where soon afterwards he became the Vice Chancellor.

But yet again, David didn't pursue his own ambition. Troubled by the violence affecting his people in the Democratic Republic of the Congo, he prayerfully quit that post. He moved back to the conflict zone to be with his people and discern what the church could do. Out of those conversations, he founded a bilingual Christian university that has been a beacon of hope for the community, *l'Université Chrétienne Bilingue du Congo*. Reflecting on his life, David says:

> My life – the way I wanted it – was to be for the first few years in the university and in the business world. But from then on, my life was as the Lord wanted it, everything I was and everything that came to me was not me fighting for it, it was just God . . . My life was surrendered to God, and then he gave me back what I was passionate about . . . if I belonged to myself, I would still be struggling and sitting somewhere doing what, I do not know.

David trusted God to provide for himself and his family. He surrendered and lived a life devoted to God and others. As a result, God has been able to use him in amazing ways.

Changed Hearts

The parable of the sheep and the goats in Matthew 25 is one of the few times Jesus addresses the final judgement that every person must face. During that final judgement, Jesus doesn't ask about miracles performed or religious services attended. He doesn't even ask about how many people we evangelized! The Judge's concern, rather, is whether people fed the hungry, clothed the poor, and cared for the sick and imprisoned. In fact, the Judge takes it so personally that it is as if they failed to care for him: "Truly I tell you, just as you did not do it to the least of these, you did not do it to me" (Matthew 25:45).

Jesus, the One before whom you and I must give an account, is not concerned about the things that vex most Christians and churches. Instead, he will be asking, "What have you done with the time, talents, and resources that I entrusted to you?" Specifically, this passage teaches us that our salvation will be demonstrated by how we served the poor and needy.

I sometimes wonder if the fear of using good works to earn our salvation has destroyed any motive for us Christians to work any good at all with our resources. Good works save no one. But one who has been reconciled to God through faith and repentance *will*, by the power of the Holy Spirit, become a fountain of good works – of love, of mercy, of generosity. In other words, our salvation transforms us into the good stewards Jesus calls us to be.

> Instead, Zacchaeus changed his life because he had met Jesus.

When Jesus said to Zacchaeus, "Today salvation has come to this house," it was because Zacchaeus had repented. He had changed his priorities, his agenda, his behaviour, and his life. He gave half of what he had to the poor, and to those whom he had defrauded, he restored fourfold what he had taken (Luke 19:1-10). Did Zacchaeus *have* to do these things in order to be saved? There is nothing in this story to indicate that earning salvation was the issue. Instead, Zacchaeus changed his life because he had met Jesus.

If we are genuinely born again, then we will bear a family likeness with our Older Brother and our heavenly Father. As the apostle John put it: "Beloved, we are God's children now; what we will be has not yet been revealed. What we do know is this: when he is revealed, we will be like him, for we will see him as he is. And all who have this hope in him purify themselves, just as he is pure" (1 John 3:2-3).

We demonstrate the reality of our faith, of our relationship with Christ, not with our religious words but by the way we love God and love our neighbours. If we are saved and are following Jesus as his disciples, it will be obvious from our joyful stewardship.

Feeding the Hungry and Visiting the Sick

Sarah was an Ethiopian Christian whose husband got sick and died. At his funeral he was hailed as a good, honourable Christian man. Not long after his death however, Sarah got sick. A blood test showed that she was HIV-positive. Both her family and her husband's family blamed her for her husband's death, but in fact, the husband had contracted HIV from visiting prostitutes, thereby infecting her and their unborn child. Because of the shame and stigma, he had never gotten tested; he didn't want to know. The relatives drove Sarah and her three children, including her HIV-positive newborn daughter, out of the house and onto the streets.

Having lost everything, she begged for food to feed her children. Members of the church where I served as senior pastor found them and gave them medical care from a team of visiting doctors. Our outreach ministry provided food and school fees for the older children. And they built a small but adequate house so Sarah and her family could have a roof over their heads.

Not long after this, the director and I went to visit Sarah and found her weak and unable to move in her bed. We thought she might be dying of AIDS. We laid our hands on her and I began praying, "In the name of Jesus . . ." She suddenly shrieked and snarled and violently thrashed about her bed. We held her down so she wouldn't hurt herself or us, and we prayed that God would deliver Sarah from what seemed to be a demonic attack. Sarah suddenly collapsed and lay still. We stayed for some time, and then left her in the care of her neighbours.

A few days later we were shocked to see Sarah walking into the director's office. She was praising God for delivering her from the demons and had come to thank us for praying for her.

Our church's practical ministry to someone who others ignored is an example of the kind of Christianity that distinguishes the sheep from the goats, and it is something any of us can do right where we are.

The Supreme Example

No matter how much or how little we have, we can be stewards of what God has given us. God is not impressed with amounts given in his name, because a rich person can give a vast amount to be seen by others as generous, and yet he has not come close to giving sacrificially.

While teaching near the place in the Temple complex where offerings were brought, Jesus directed his disciples to watch carefully. Wealthy people put in large sums, but a poor widow put in only two coins. Jesus said, "Truly I tell you, this poor widow has put in more than all of them; for all of them have contributed out of their abundance, but she out of her poverty has put in all she had to live on" (Luke 21:3-4).

She gave what she had, not so that anyone would see her, but just to express to the Lord that she was his and trusting him to provide what she needed. Two copper coins made no significant increase whatsoever in the Temple's budget. But heaven had not seen a gift so substantial in a very long time.

The Ethiopian Widow's Gift

The story of the widow's gift at the Temple reminds me of what happened next with Sarah, the HIV-positive widow mentioned in the story above. About a month after Sarah was delivered from the demonic attack, a newborn baby was left at the church's gate. The infant was probably HIV-positive, which meant that nobody would want her. In those days an HIV-positive child might live five or six years but would grow sick and weak and inevitably die. Our ministry director circulated the need for someone who could care for this baby while we searched for a long-term solution.

The next day, Sarah came by the director's office again. "I want to take care of that little girl," she said.

"Why?" the director asked. "You already have three children to take care of."

> "After all God has done for me, how can I not give what I have?"

"Yes," said Sarah, "but I know how to take care of children, even sick children. And besides, after all God has done for me, how can I not give what I have to take care of this little girl who desperately needs someone to love her and be a family for her?"

Sarah took the infant home. I have since moved from Ethiopia and have lost track of Sarah and her family. But she brings to life for me just what a poor widow's two mites can do. The poor woman who had nothing in the world's eyes is now showing people what love is, what gratitude does, and what it means to be a good steward.

It All Belongs to God

What we see again and again in the Gospels is that Jesus wants to rescue us from the ways of this world and reclaim us for his kingdom. He knows if we persist in our love of money, we will destroy ourselves. Jesus's hard words about stewardship offer us the way of life on the narrow road to salvation. If our lives and churches are impoverished in the things of God, it is because, ironically, too many of us feel we have too much to lose if we take stewardship seriously.

Whether we call it the "lordship of Christ" or "stewardship", the biblical concept is precisely the same. Everything we have and everything we are belongs to Christ. Not just a few coins, not just 10 per cent, but *everything*. So, we need to use everything he places in our hands, every talent and ability, for the sake of his agenda and glory.

Jesus lays claim to all of our lives and confronts us with the call to follow him. The primary means by which we love both God and our neighbour is not with our words, but with what we have been given by God – our time and our talents and our treasure. This is why our relationship with our material possessions shows, more clearly than any other indicator, the true direction of our lives.

CHAPTER SIX

After Jesus: Stewardship in First-Century Christianity

In high school, I heard a sermon threatening me with the fire of hell unless I trusted in Jesus to forgive my sins. I knew I had not lived well. A friend had recently died, so I had been thinking a lot about death. I prayed to receive Jesus as my personal Saviour.

Then I asked some of my new Christian friends, "Now what? What do Christians do?" They told me to go to church; find a ministry with which to get involved; don't smoke or drink or gamble; and don't have sex until after marriage. This seemed like a small vision for following God.

In my first year at university, I attended a weekend retreat for students in Christian fellowships from universities in the region. The main speaker gave a talk on the lordship of Christ. The speaker was saying that Jesus doesn't just come and save us from hell so we can go off to heaven when we die. Jesus calls us to follow him *now*, to give ourselves and our talents and our time and possessions to him right *now*. "We don't add Jesus onto our life," he said. "We join our life with his!"

It shook me at my core. Afterwards, I went on a walk by myself to think through what I had heard. Although I had known I could turn to Jesus when I needed help, I must admit I was that person the speaker was talking about, who understood Jesus to be an add-on to the life I wanted to live. Despite knowing the right things to say and being seen as a young Christian leader, I had used Jesus to meet my needs and pursue my agenda.

But now I saw Christianity wasn't about Jesus meeting my needs. Instead I needed to surrender everything to Christ, so that Christ might enable me to become more and more like him.

I was never the same again after that night. I voraciously read the Scriptures, understanding with new eyes what God wants to do in our world. The Gospels and their stories of Jesus were compelling. When I reached the Book of Acts, I began to find some answers to my question about what it looked like to live as Christians. I saw what it looked like when a community took Jesus seriously, how God intervened in amazing ways among them, and how they grew in faith, love, and numbers. I wondered why our churches were satisfied with so little when God could do so much. I wanted to know this radical Christianity.

Not long afterward, I understood God was calling me to be a missionary. With both fear and joy, I threw myself into getting the training I needed to serve Christ in cross-cultural ministry. And that is where I still am today, after all these decades.

Following Through

When we say Jesus is our Lord, it means fully surrendering to Christ. The Christians in Acts recognized that their lives were no longer their own – everything they were and had was a gift from God.

Jesus's teaching about stewardship was not an idealized version that the first Christians quickly dismissed. The early Christians did not feel at liberty to ignore the aspects of Jesus's teaching they didn't like. Instead, in their lives and communities they earnestly attempted to reproduce Jesus's teachings about money and stewardship, passed on to them by the apostles.

Luke's summary statements in the early chapters of Acts are striking:

> They devoted themselves to the apostles' teaching and fellowship, to the breaking of bread and the prayers.
>
> Awe came upon everyone, because many wonders and signs were being done by the apostles. All who believed were together and had all things in common; they would sell their possessions and goods and distribute the proceeds to all, as any had need. Day by day as they spent much time together in the temple, they broke bread at home and ate their food with glad and generous hearts, praising God and having the goodwill of all the people. And day by day the Lord added to their number those who were being saved (Acts 2:42-47 NRSV-A).

And again, after some time had passed:

> Now the whole group of those who believed were of one heart and soul, and no one claimed private ownership of any possessions, but everything they owned was held in common. With great power the apostles gave their testimony to the resurrection of the Lord Jesus, and great grace was upon them all. There was not a needy person among them, for as many as owned lands or houses sold them and brought the proceeds of what was sold. They laid it at the apostles' feet and it was distributed to each as any had need (Acts 4:32-35).

It is easy for us to pick our way carefully through these passages to avoid their impact. For example, F. Scott Spencer writes, "Of course, however much we might admire the radical communitarian practice of the early Jerusalem church, we may also pity, even decry, their shortsighted, impractical economic vision. Quite possibly, it contributed to hard times down the line, requiring assistance (bailout) from the more prosperous congregation in Antioch (11:27-30)." Yet Spencer still ends by warning that dismissing the early church's practice risks "dismissing their vibrant resurrection faith that ignited their extraordinary common-fellowship *(koinonia)* in the first place. And resurrection faith that does not profoundly shape communal practice lacks depth of meaning and breadth of appeal."[19]

Depending on our political leanings, we might also disparage the practices of the early Jerusalem church by associating them with communism.[20] For instance, Jason Jackson is quick to clarify that unlike a Marxist-forced redistribution of wealth, the members of the church still owned pieces of land or homes and sold property voluntarily. The property was distributed to the needy – not everyone, and not people who refused to work.[21] But Jackson's concerns are based on comparing these practices with a secular economic theory that didn't emerge for another 1,800 years.

If we dismiss the community life of a first-century church because we think it's too similar to economic and political ideologies from the 19th and 20th centuries, we are ignorant at best. At worst, we are trying to justify not taking seriously the example of the first Christians.[22]

> What these first Christians were doing was completely consistent with what Jesus had been teaching just a few months and years before.

Of the many things that could be said about these passages, one thing stands out: What these first Christians were doing was completely consistent with what Jesus had been teaching just a few months and years before. In other words, the Jerusalem church was not suddenly devising a new economic policy. Rather, the community was motivated by one driving concern – to give help to the needy among them.[23] And a straight line can be drawn from their concern for the poor back to Jesus himself. They took seriously what Jesus had said the night he was betrayed: "I give you a new commandment, that you love one another. Just as I have loved you, you also should love one another. By this everyone will know that you are my disciples, if you have love for one another" (John 13:34-35).

And so, when they came across instances of need within the community, they took steps to help. As a result, "There was not a needy person among them" (Acts 4:34a). Given the size of the early Christian movement, this is quite a remarkable thing for Luke to say.

This was not a momentary emphasis of the first Christians. The apostles were focused and serious about facilitating the care of the marginalized among them throughout their lives. And it required more than just individual charity; the entire community was mobilized to see this as a crucial aspect of their discipleship and their mission as a church. Relatively early on, they created a methodology to ensure that none of the truly needy in the church were overlooked.

But the day came when, despite their best efforts, some among them were overlooked; widows amongst the Hellenist Christians "were being neglected in the daily distribution of food" (Acts 6:1). First of all, it's worth noticing that there *was* a daily distribution for the needy in the community. Anyone who has worked in a soup kitchen or a food pantry for the poor knows the level of organization and effort required to be effective.

Second, it took so much effort that the apostles came to admit that they could not continue to run the ministry themselves. Grumblings that Greek-speaking widows were being overlooked in the distribution of food were taken seriously. The apostles were evidently stretched thin and overwhelmed. Moreover, the burden of administering charity was so significant that the apostles felt they were being increasingly kept away from their mission of evangelism and teaching.

Hence a new level of community leadership was created to take responsibility for the programmes that would implement Jesus's teaching about love, giving, and the poor. The selection of deacons in Acts 6 indicates the extent of the charity being practised by the Jerusalem community.[24] Considering that seven men were selected to administer this ministry, we can see just how substantial was the effort by the church to take care of the needy in Jerusalem.

Feeding the Hungry

I knew of a church where a woman happened to be studying the Book of Acts during her personal Bible study and prayer time. When she read in chapter 6 about how the apostles dealt with the need to better administer the Jerusalem church's charitable ministries to the poor in their midst, she realized her church could be spending its resources more faithfully in this regard. She soon came up with a plan.

First, she got the church board's permission to use the church's kitchen facilities and one of its Sunday school classrooms to start a healthy meal centre that would provide a hot, nutritious lunch every Wednesday. She recruited several other church ladies to volunteer their time and prepare the meals. She and another friend put up the money for the first month. They advertised by word of mouth, asking church members to invite the elderly, the infirm, and any poor people they knew, both from within the church or outside it, to come and share a free meal on Wednesday at noon.

On the first Wednesday, to everyone's surprise, 20 people came. The next week the number doubled, and the kitchen staff struggled to have enough for everyone. The third week, nearly 80 came. They had to open two more classrooms to make room for everybody. By this time, church members were responding with offerings; others contributed plates and utensils and cups. More people volunteered to help the mamas in the kitchen. By the end of the first month, not only were more than 100 of the city's disadvantaged people coming to the church on Wednesday for lunch, but nearly 20 of the church's members were mobilized to plan, shop, prepare, serve, and clean up.

When the woman who had started all this looked over the crowd of people sitting in classrooms and outside on the ground eating their lunch and others in line patiently waiting to be served, she suddenly realized what she was looking at. No longer was she seeing poor people, instead she saw men who were unemployed, needing a hand to get through this hard time. She saw young mothers with infants in their arms and small children in tow, grateful for a warm, filling meal. She saw street boys who, at least for an hour, had something positive to focus on. She saw elderly women who came at the insistence of their neighbours, both to get out of the house and also get something healthy to eat. She saw other men who were notorious town drunks, but who in this hour at least put off their addiction and had positive contact with other people. All of them were fellow human beings – and that by helping them, the church was fulfilling its calling.

The elders were astonished at the impact of a simple meal on both the lives of a growing circle of people and on the church. Several of them volunteered their time and money. The wife of an elder volunteered her time as a counsellor and began to meet with whoever wanted to talk. She was soon so overwhelmed by the sheer numbers of people wanting help with their challenges that she talked several of her colleagues into volunteering some hours every week to come and help.

By the end of the year, the board of elders had constructed a new kitchen big enough to handle the number of meals being prepared. They also built a large hall that could accommodate the large number of people who showed up. They brought on a director to better organize the process and provided offices for five or six counsellors to use. And they began serving lunch on Fridays as well. Church members and leaders were encouraged to simply come and get to know a new person every week. The poor or struggling in the community knew that on Wednesday and Friday they could get not only a hot meal, but they could come to a safe place where they were not judged but rather accepted as fellow human beings created in the image of God.

None of this would have happened, however, if not for one woman who took the example of the early church seriously and decided to do something.

Follow the Money

While coming up with an effective administrative system was a challenge for the apostles, funding was also an issue for their new and growing churches, just as it is for most churches today. Luke tells us that: "There was a Levite, a native of Cyprus, Joseph, to whom the apostles gave the name Barnabas (which means 'son of encouragement'). He sold a field that belonged to him, then brought the money and laid it at the apostles' feet" (Acts 4:34-37).

> Funding was also an issue for their new and growing churches, just as it is for most churches today.

We don't know how many in the Jerusalem church were choosing to give in this way. We also don't know the extent of the need in the Jerusalem church, nor do we know if the help they received went beyond food and rent to help people also find work and affordable housing. What we do know is that the help given by the Jerusalem Christians was substantial and that it met the needs of the community, though at considerable cost.

Persecution scattered the Jerusalem church, and the Christian movement spread. Former persecutor Saul converted, and the rest of Acts describes Saul, who takes the name Paul, as he travels as a missionary and establishes churches throughout the Gentile Roman world.

The transition from pagan assumptions and a Greek worldview was challenging for the new Gentile Christians across the Mediterranean. It included a necessary change in mindset towards money, generosity, and stewardship. Most of the apostolic input on giving and stewardship occurred when the community was gathered to hear the apostles teach, or to hear their letters read. These covered the entire range of Christian issues, from Jesus and the gospel, to worship and sacraments, and matters of appropriate conduct and living out one's faith.

We learn from Paul's letter to the Romans that the church in Jerusalem had been enduring a particularly difficult time. He informs the Roman Christians that, before he can visit them in Rome, he must go to Jerusalem:

> I do hope to see you on my journey [when I go to Spain] and to be sent on by you, once I have enjoyed your company for a little while. At present, however, I am going to Jerusalem in a ministry to the saints; for Macedonia and Achaia have been pleased to share their resources with the poor among the saints at Jerusalem (Romans 15:24-26).

We learn from Paul's correspondence with the church in Corinth that not a little persuasion was necessary to motivate them to participate. Near the end of his first letter he writes:

Now concerning the collection for the saints: you should follow the directions I gave to the churches of Galatia. On the first day of every week, each of you is to put aside and save whatever extra you earn, so that collections need not be taken when I come. And when I arrive, I will send any whom you approve with letters to take your gift to Jerusalem. If it seems advisable that I should go also, they will accompany me (1 Corinthians 16:1-4).

But as the time draws near to actually collect the money and deliver it to Jerusalem, Paul finds he needs to nudge the Corinthians to follow through on what they evidently had agreed to do. Here is Paul's undergirding principle, presumably with all the Greek churches, on this issue of stewardship:

The point is this: the one who sows sparingly will also reap sparingly, and the one who sows bountifully will also reap bountifully. Each of you must give as you have made up your mind, not reluctantly or under compulsion, for God loves a cheerful giver. And God is able to provide you with every blessing in abundance, so that so that by always having enough of everything, you may share abundantly in every good work. As it is written,

'He scatters abroad, he gives to the poor;
  his righteousness endures for ever' (2 Corinthians 9:6-9).

The principle of sowing and reaping has been misused among preachers and ministers nowadays to encourage congregants to give money to their ministries. They say that the more people give (sow) the more they will get (reap). Congregants give large amounts of money, expecting multiples in financial returns, or a lucrative business deal, or success in all their endeavours as interest on their investment. But this takes New Testament teaching on money out of context and makes our stewardship into simply another way to get access to money. For Jesus and Paul, it's not about using God to get rich; it's about giving as a way to demonstrate love, and without any hope of any return other than gratitude. We cannot manipulate God into making us wealthy. What Paul is trying to say here is that God is able to provide you with enough *to do the good things he has called you to do*, including giving to others who are in need. While people who misuse this Scripture today make people focus on getting more money for themselves, Paul's point is that Christians should not be concerned with getting God's blessing, but rather with being God's blessing to those in need around them.

Christians of all people can afford to be generous, according to Paul, not least because of how generous God is to us in Christ. But Christian generosity is undergirded by the added promises that God will provide for his people *precisely in order* that they might be generous.

By participating in this ministry of giving, the Corinthians are to demonstrate that they are a part of God's new community. The self-centred parochial concerns that each one brings to the table will be transformed. Giving will demonstrate their love, which will also bear witness to the reality of their new life in Christ.

There is another New Testament hint of what stewardship looks like (or doesn't look like) in the early church. Paul, in his letter to the Christians in Philippi, commends them for supporting him financially as he engaged in further missionary work – even though other churches had not.

This tells us that stewardship did not come naturally to the first generation of Christians – just as it doesn't come naturally to Christians today. Paul condemns no one for this slowness. Nor is he seeking to get rich off the kindness of others. Instead he views his own needs in apostolic ministry as an opportunity for others to excel in the blessing of giving, promising that "my God will fully satisfy every need of yours according to his riches in glory in Christ Jesus" (Philippians 4:19).

Christian stewardship prompts Christians to be a channel of the blessings God has given us. Paul states that as we give of what God has given us, God will not only provide what we need but will entrust us with even more to give in his name. God doesn't satisfy our greedy desires or bankroll an extravagant lifestyle. But when we align ourselves with his priorities and give ourselves sacrificially for the sake of his kingdom, God will bless and enable us as his people to do what he calls us to do.

What Is "Pure Religion"?

James, the first bishop of the Jerusalem church, provides further evidence of how closely Christian belief was tied to Christian behaviour in general and Christian charity in particular. In his characteristically blunt way, James simply says: "Religion that is pure and undefiled before God, the Father, is this: to care for orphans and widows in their distress, and to keep oneself unstained by the world" (James 1:27). When James brings up the issue of genuine faith as opposed to its counterfeit, he chooses an example that has to do with the needy:

> What good is it, my brothers and sisters, if you say you have faith but do not have works? Can faith save you? If a brother or sister is naked and lacks daily food, and one of you says to them, 'Go in peace; keep warm, and eat your fill', and yet you do not supply their bodily needs, what is the good of that? So faith by itself, if it has no works, is dead (James 2:14-17).

James makes our use of material possessions – our stewardship – a matter of our fundamental standing before God. In this case, works are what we choose to do with what we have. It would not be a stretch to say that, for James, faith without stewardship is dead.

When ideas about stewardship surface in the New Testament epistles, they emerge fully formed and with passion. Churches gave towards ongoing feeding for needy widows and orphans or one-time donations to feed distant congregations in famine. They supported their giving with leadership structures, developed fundraising campaigns, and delegated trustworthy individuals to follow up.

> James makes our use of material possessions – our stewardship – a matter of our fundamental standing before God.

What we *don't* see in the New Testament is a church *not* thinking about money or stewardship. Instead, these early believers are fully engaged with supporting local ministers and ministries, and fully capable of responding to extraordinary needs as they arise. The evidence suggests that Jewish and Gentile churches treated the teachings of Jesus or the apostles on matters of money and stewardship as what they were expected to do too. The quick snapshots of the churches bear this out.

Later, when the number of Christians increased enough to be noticed, they acquired the reputation of taking care of the poor and needy. By the time their neighbours began to take Christians seriously, stewardship was their habit, the default position of individual Christians and local churches. We can now begin to see why eminent sociologist Rodney Stark explains that cities in the Greco-Roman world were miserable places, but Christian relationships gave new life to those cities:

> To cities filled with the homeless and impoverished, Christianity offered charity as well as hope. To cities filled with newcomers and strangers, Christianity offered an immediate basis for attachment. To cities filled with orphans and widows, Christianity

provided a new and expanded sense of family. To cities torn by violent ethnic strife, Christianity offered a new basis for social solidarity . . . And to cities faced with epidemics, fires, and earthquakes, Christianity offered effective nursing services . . . For what they brought was not simply an urban movement, but a new culture capable of making life in Greco-Roman cities more tolerable.[25]

Of course, the early Christians had their issues and even scandals, like churches today. But the way they dealt with their money and resources was different enough from the surrounding cultures to attract attention, and most likely new converts as well.

Not Impossible after All

It's sad how many Christians believe it's impossible to live like the early church. Our own unwillingness to change doesn't change whether the Scriptures themselves are true or God's call is valid! So we remain with our persistent poverty and corruption instead of the vision of a Christian community we see in Acts. When it comes to being God's blessing for our community, we are too often our own worst enemies.

Instead of getting discouraged, think what can happen if a few of us took up the challenge and lived out this vision! The woman I described with the vision of feeding some hungry people had a different experience. She felt challenged by what she read in Acts, and she saw a small need that she could do something about. She didn't wait for outside help. She just did what was in front of her to do. And she made a difference – in the lives of the disadvantaged in her church, and even in her own life as her own faith was challenged week by week.

Stewardship is never just about money, it's about transformation – the transformation of our lives as we become God's blessing in the lives of others, and the transformation of our churches into the very presence and power of Jesus in our communities. I have focused on how Christians have responded to the poor in their midst, but there are many other ways stewardship was expressed in Acts and will be expressed in your church and in your experience. The fundamental issue is simply: am I ready to put all that I have and all that I am at the Lord's disposal for him to use for his glory? That's stewardship. That's God's goal for us as his born-again children. That's God's goal for us as his church.

CHAPTER SEVEN

A Great Cloud of Witnesses

And what happened when those first apostles, who had heard Jesus's teaching on stewardship from his own mouth, departed this life? Did the first-century Christians begin to change with the passing of time?

Fortunately for us, many texts written by leaders and writers from the first millennium have survived. These documents give glimpses into the lives and priorities of their times. As we shall see, issues of money and stewardship were just as important to Christians and their churches then as they are now. We will also notice that the idea of stewardship in the early church was always about much more than just tithing. None of the writings that survive from the first 150 years of Christianity suggest either a monetary or percentage amount that Christians should give, but they show radical sacrifice and great concern for the poor. In chapter four, we quoted Irenaeus, the Bishop of Lyon at the end of the second century, describing Jesus's teaching in the Gospels and the practice of New Testament Christians:

> They [O.T. saints] offered their tithes; but those who have received liberty set apart everything they have for the Lord's

use, cheerfully and freely giving them (2 Corinthians 9:7), not as small things in the hope of greater, but like that poor widow, who put her whole livelihood into the treasury of God (Luke 21:4).[26]

As we will see, in the first five centuries of the church, people really lived out these convictions. Christians were giving sacrificially and cheerfully for the sake of the poor, for the sake of the church, and to advance the gospel and the Kingdom of God.

The Didache

One of the earliest writings we have, called *The Teaching of the Twelve Apostles*, or the *Didache* (a Greek noun meaning "teaching"), is a kind of church manual. It was apparently written by an unknown member of that second generation of Christian writers we call the Apostolic Fathers, perhaps as early as the mid to late first century. In one striking passage, it states:

> Do not be one who holds his hand out to take, but shuts it when it comes to giving . . . for you will discover who [God] is that pays you back a reward with a good grace. Do not turn your back on the needy, but share everything with your brother and call nothing your own. For if you have what is eternal in common, how much more should you have what is transient! (*Didache* 4:5-8).[27]

If you have what is eternal in common, how much more should you have what is transient!

This paragraph echoes what the early Jerusalem church did in Acts 2 and 4, who knew that if they already shared things that will last forever, they should certainly be willing to share the things on earth.

Christian generosity and hospitality give evidence of one's salvation, but they are not to be abused. Apparently, early Christians encountered many travellers claiming to be this or that person of importance in the church. Christians are to be generous, the *Didache* says, but not gullible:

> Welcome every apostle on arriving, as if he were the Lord. But he must not stay beyond one day. In case of necessity, however, the next day too. If he stays three days, he is a false prophet. On departing, an apostle must not accept anything save sufficient food to carry him till his next lodging. If he asks for money, he is a false prophet (*Didache* 11:3-6).

The next chapter gives the same guidelines for other Christian visitors travelling through. After three days, the guest must work for his living in a trade or help the host in other ways. *Didache* 12:1-5 warns: "If he refuses to do this, he is trading on Christ. You must be on your guard against such people." The fact that the author speaks against these things tells us that such abusers of Christian generosity were somewhat common.

Today we see many claiming to be men or women of God. Perhaps they come to your village and expect to be hosted. They begin having services and extracting offerings. But too often there is no accountability. Too often their titles are self-generated.

There are legitimate evangelists and pastors called by God into a sacrificial ministry among God's people. Welcoming them and supporting their ministry is an act of service to God and to the church. But some people today, just as during the time of the *Didache*, are in it for the money and taking advantage of Christians. We should be cautious of people who expect others to support them and use spiritual threats if anyone challenges their authority.

If we followed the *Didache's* advice and removed money from the equation, I wonder how many of these so-called apostles, prophets, and servants of God would stay around?

Clement of Alexandria

Clement of Alexandria (AD 150-215) was an African convert to Christianity. He taught at the Catechetical School in Alexandria and influenced a long line of remarkable leaders from the church in Egypt.

Alexandria was the second city of the Roman Empire, and the emperor Hadrian declared that the Alexandrians were "mutinous, empty-headed and troublesome; their city is rich, wealthy and prosperous; everyone is busy; their only god is money."[28]

In this context, Clement wrote a small treatise, *Can a Rich Man Be Saved?* Clement believes a rich man can, in fact be saved, but he goes further and explains how Christians should use money. He explains what Jesus meant in his Sermon on the Mount when he said: "Blessed are the poor in spirit, for theirs is the kingdom of heaven" (Matthew 5:3 NRSV-A). People who are "poor in spirit" see their possessions as gifts God has given them to save others and for the sake of others. Their focus is on doing good work, so they will be equally cheerful if they lose their possessions.[29] But the rich person who cannot be saved is the one who "carries his riches in his soul, and instead of God's Spirit bears in his heart gold or land." His focus is on always getting more possessions on earth, so he can't possibly focus on the kingdom of heaven. "For where the mind of a man is, there is also his treasure," Clement paraphrases.[30]

Our culture's view of money may not be very different from Alexandria's long ago. Are your peers absorbed by trying to get ahead, making investments, and buying luxury items? Does your family or your community pressure you to be successful by your culture's definition? Clement is an excellent example of a Christian leader who didn't give in to pressure. Despite living in a city where everyone's god was money, Clement refused to follow his culture's expectations. He challenged Christians under his leadership to live by a different set of values. He observed that riches were generally toxic to the faith handed down from the apostles. The only escape was to use one's riches in a *Christian* way, meeting the needs of others with the plenty one has. Take his challenge to heart and consider: how much of your mind do you devote to money and how much time do you spend thinking about serving God and others?

Marcus Minucius Felix

The early Christians were a mostly poor, sometimes persecuted minority. But the way they lived caught the attention of their neighbours. Some pagans viewed Christian poverty as a sign of weakness or even wickedness. A Christian named Marcus Minucius Felix (died circa AD 250 in Rome)[31] responded that Christians should be admired, not shamed, for their poverty, because it strengthened their character. The truly poor in his view were those who always felt they didn't have enough possessions. But Christians without material possessions were not poor, because they were content with what they had, including having God's presence. Marcus said: "When a man walks along a road, the lighter he travels, the happier he is; equally, on this journey of life, a man is more blessed if he does not pant beneath a burden of riches but lightens his load by poverty." If Christians needed anything, they could ask the God who owns everything, but Marcus believed what Christians really wanted to ask God for was innocence, patience, and goodness.[32]

Most Christians on the continent of Africa are poor. Some so-called Christian prophets and apostles would like to make us feel ashamed of our poverty when we see their lavish lifestyles, fancy cars and houses, and even private jets. Successful but corrupt businessmen or politicians may also look down on us Christians who are poor because we refuse to cheat others. Sometimes we may even wonder if we are cursed. But really the people who are becoming wealthy unjustly are the ones bringing judgement on themselves. Although it is an unpopular opinion, Marcus reminds us that we can be grateful that we have few possessions, finding our contentment in God as he grows our character.

> Really the people who are becoming wealthy unjustly are the ones bringing judgement on themselves.

Cyprian of Carthage

The African bishop Cyprian of Carthage (in modern day Tunisia) reflects on the causes behind the defection of so many Christians during the persecutions of mid-third century North Africa. Cyprian says many had lost their first love for Christ. Instead, they had become passionate about acquiring more and more wealth. "Gone was the devotion of bishops to the service of God, gone was the clergy's faithful integrity, gone the generous compassion for the needy, gone all discipline in our behaviour." He specifically points out:

> Too many bishops, instead of giving encouragement and example to others, [ignored the ministry] which God had entrusted to them ... took up the administration of secular business: they ... abandoned their people, and toured the markets in other territories on the look-out for profitable deals. If that is what we have become, what do we not deserve for such sins?[33]

Does this sound like some of the bishops, pastors, priests, prophets, and apostles who have set up shop in churches and ministries all across our continent? There is a huge office and shopping building recently constructed on one of the main roads in Nairobi called the "Bishop M— Building". The man has certainly made a name for himself. But has he glorified God's name? If we have their words and actions to guide us, these false teachers seem much more concerned to make money for themselves and for their schemes than to be genuine disciples of Christ. If these are our shepherds, where will they lead the sheep?

Monks, Deserts, and Stewardship

Christianity was granted official toleration under Roman Emperor Constantine's Edict of Milan (AD 313), which officially ended the last bloody spasm of state-sponsored persecution. When it became clear that Constantine himself may actually have become a Christian, joining a church began to be seen as a way of upward mobility, increasing one's chance for a good government job. Christianity became popular and churches were flooded with people who called themselves Christians but not all were true followers of Jesus.

As many wealthy, powerful, and worldly people joined the church, more seriously minded Christians fled into the desert to get away from worldly corruption. They wanted to pursue fundamental Christian spirituality. The monastic movement eventually became the source of much spiritual formation, missions, scholarship, and leadership. From the very beginning, the monks and nuns of Egypt, Palestine, and Syria emphasized the necessity of both poverty and charity.

There are many stories of the early desert fathers and mothers (monks and nuns) responding to God's call on their lives by giving away their possessions to the poor and simply trusting God to provide. I have already told the account of Anthony (in chapter five). The monks' life of simplicity could not have contrasted more with the over-the-top displays of wealth and power in the city churches. Their poverty prophetically called people to repent from loving power and wealth.

City-dwelling Christians began to seek out these monks of the desert as spiritual guides. Some of this was a kind of religious tourism; other people had more legitimate motives. Many of the desert fathers began to feel they were too close to town and it was too easy to find them. So they moved to even more remote locations.

Monasticism continued to spread into Asia Minor, Italy, and Gaul, then onward into Ireland and Britain. Today, there is still a huge monastic movement in Ethiopia among members of the Ethiopian Orthodox church, which is the oldest and longest surviving Christian church in sub-Saharan Africa. There are communities of monks and nuns scattered in almost every African country – Roman Catholic, Orthodox, and even Anglican – who have left material possessions in order to be free to do their ministries of charity and teaching.

Basil of Caesarea

As the monastic movement was expanding in the fourth century, monks were increasingly seen as appropriate candidates to become bishops. In some cases, of course, the perks and power of these positions could erode their character and morality. But in other cases, the men selected as bishop of a particular area, town, or city saw the churches there respond with true renewal and even revival.

One such bishop was Basil of Caesarea (circa AD 330-379). He preached a sermon about Christian stewardship, probably in 368, when Asia Minor (Turkey) was experiencing a severe drought and shortage of food. Some of the rich were holding back grain in order to force the prices even higher. (It reminds me of when there was a shortage of maize flour in Kenya, and some mills were withholding the flour they had to try and get a better price.)

In Basil's congregation, there were suffering men, women, and children, as well as people who had plenty but were doing nothing to help those in desperate need. Basil was justifiably angry. He preached: " 'Who am I injuring,' you will say, 'when I keep what is mine for myself?' And what, tell me, is yours? And from where have you brought it with you into this life?" If God has given resources to you and not to others, Basil argued, it is not because God is unjust, but because he is giving you an opportunity to earn rewards for being compassionate, patient, and stewarding your resources well.[34]

"If each took only what was sufficient for his needs, and left what remained, there would be no rich and no poor," Basil pointed out.[35] If you are not content with enough and you keep more than you need when others need it, Basil says you will be judged:

> That bread you hold in your clutches, that belongs to the starving. That cloak you keep locked away in your wardrobe, that belongs to the naked. Those shoes that are going to waste with you, they belong to the barefooted. That silver you buried away, that belongs to the needy. Whomsoever you could have helped and did not, to so many you have been unjust.[36]

In the previous chapter, we mentioned how the Hebrew word for giving alms also meant righteousness, because it was only giving the poor what belonged to them. Basil's words may sound strong, but they are very biblical.

I am surrounded by people who have much less than I have. I cannot open my closet and look at my many pairs of shoes without thinking of what Bishop Basil said to the wealthy members of his church. Nor can I look into my cupboard with all my choices of things to eat without thinking of those who have nothing. What about you? What things do you have more than enough of? Who in your community might need some of these things that God has put in your care to distribute?

Ambrose

Meanwhile in the Western part of the Roman Empire, Ambrose (circa AD 340-397) was the son of a high-ranking political figure. He had been brought up in a Christian family and had risen to prominence as a gifted civil administrator and governor of Milan.

Then the bishop of Milan died. This led to a spasm of civil strife, during which the people fixed on Ambrose to be their bishop, even though he wasn't even a priest. After going into hiding, he sensed God's call and allowed himself to be ordained.

As a bishop, Ambrose immediately adopted the simple lifestyle of an ascetic. After ensuring a living for his sister, he gave his possessions to the poor, donated his land to the church, and entrusted his family into the care of his brother. Because of these personal choices, Ambrose was viewed as a man who spoke with integrity and whose life matched his rhetoric.

> He gave his possessions to the poor, donated his land to the church, and entrusted his family into the care of his brother.

As with Basil in the East, Ambrose repeatedly clashed with Christians in his diocese who felt they could have it all, both worldly treasure and spiritual security. In his sermon on 1 Kings 21 (circa 395), Ambrose explained that the earth was made for everyone, so how can rich people claim exclusive rights to the soil? From nature's perspective, we are naked when we are born and when we die.[37] Therefore, he found the difference between rich and poor unjust: "The people are starving, and you close your barns; the people weep bitterly, and you toy with a jewelled ring . . . The jewel in your ring could preserve the lives of the whole people."

According to Ambrose, someone who was unable to give their inheritance to the poor showed that they were a servant to their wealth instead of mastering it. In such a case, "the man belongs to his riches, not the riches to the man."[38]

Inheritance is very important in many of cultures in Africa. In some cases, families can be divided and stop speaking for years because of conflicts over inheritance. But when we see the example of Ambrose, we see that he was more concerned with his eternal security than his financial security. Could you donate your inherited land to the church? Could you give up a prominent government post to serve God's people? As Christian leaders today, the power of our message will be most visible in the way it is changing our own lives. Do we show by the way we live that following Christ is worth *everything*?

Augustine

Ambrose's reputation as a preacher with spiritual integrity drew a North African seeker on the fringes of Christianity into his congregation. Augustine (AD 354-430) had dabbled in different religious beliefs and become sceptical. He had moved from Carthage to Rome and then to Milan, where he had been given a prestigious position teaching rhetoric. Augustine was attracted to Bishop Ambrose's rhetorical skills. Soon Augustine began to take seriously what the bishop was preaching. Eventually, Augustine embraced Christianity.

Shortly before his conversion, Augustine had been reading about the life of Anthony the desert father. He was already acquainted with the lifestyle choices of his spiritual patron Ambrose. So it is not surprising that Augustine himself chose to adopt the simple life of a monk when he finally moved back to the North African town of Hippo. He became a bishop there and is still remembered as one of the greatest leaders of the early church.

In the West today, many consider eschewing private possessions to be a kind of Marxist heresy, but among the early Christians it was viewed as the way to follow Christ and to gain an eternal inheritance in the life to come. Augustine argued that lawsuits, quarrels, and even murder come from our private property ownership. He said: "What are we fighting over? Over the things we call our own. We do not go to law about things we possess in common, do we? We all breathe in the air that belongs to all of us, and we all enjoy the sunshine that is common to all."

Augustine said Christians should focus on making a place for the Lord to dwell, so we must avoid becoming attached to private possessions, which will distract us from loving Christ.[39] He contrasted genuine Christian spirituality with materialism. Anything that shuts the door in Christ's face must be avoided at all costs; he observed that material possessions and property often do just that. If that is radical to our ears, it is because of the materialistic culture we live in, not because it isn't in the Bible. In the Gospels themselves, Jesus said pointedly that one cannot serve both God and earthly wealth. New Testament Christianity, as well as the Christianity of the early church, viewed divestment of one's possessions as one of the great fruits of genuine Christian spirituality.

There were, of course, the practical benefits to sharing property – the poor in one's community were cared for, and legitimate needs could be addressed. But the main point, which emerges again and again, is that believing one's possessions belong completely to God and using them accordingly is simply good for one's soul. Life is about more than possessions, and we cannot enter into the life of Christ whilst dragging a pile of earthly goods.

In my part of Africa land ownership is the goal of acquiring wealth. Land is valuable capital in countries with growing populations and often produces returns even in uncertain economies, similar to how people in the West view the stock market. Unfortunately, we have a huge problem with land-grabbing, that is, using bribes to alter official records so that your land is now actually mine. So much cultural pressure is put upon us to get land that many do not see how this form of materialism corrodes our hearts. People regularly choose to be something other than Christian when it comes to getting and holding on to land. But what good is it, Jesus asks us, if we gain the whole world (and all its land) but forfeit our soul? (Matthew 16:26). What Augustine taught, indeed what Christ taught, cuts across our cultures with regard to land, stocks, possessions, and wealth.

John Chrysostom

The last of the early church leaders we will consider in this survey is John Chrysostom (circa AD 349-407), Bishop of Constantinople. (*Chrysostom* means 'golden-mouthed' in view of his eloquent, powerful, biblical preaching.) John is yet another example of a Christian who abandoned his wealth and property for the sake of obeying Christ. His commitment to self-inflicted poverty infused his preaching and produced powerful calls for his hearers to follow the example of Christ and the apostles in their own lives.

In one sermon on the Rich Man and Lazarus (Luke 16:19-31), John points out that the rich man is tortured after death, seemingly judged like a thief even though he did not take anything from Lazarus, but simply because he did not share with him.[40] John quotes other Scriptures to make his point that "when we do not show mercy, we will be punished just like those who steal. For our money is the Lord's, however we may have gathered it."[41] Indeed, this last sentence is the principle at the heart of both Christian stewardship and Christian charity: what we have is not our own, but given for us to use.

John powerfully communicated the teaching of the Scriptures. He felt he was merely passing on to his hearers, not what they wanted to hear, but what the Word of God was actually saying:

> God has allowed you to have more: not for you to waste on prostitutes, drink, fancy food, expensive clothes, and all the other kinds of indolence, but for you to distribute to those in need. Just as an official in the imperial treasury, if he neglects to distribute where he is ordered, but spends instead for his own indolence, pays the penalty and is put to death, so also the rich man is a kind of steward of the money which is owed for distribution to the poor. He is directed to distribute it to his fellow servants who are in want. So, if he spends more on himself than his need requires, he will pay the harshest penalty hereafter. For his own goods are not his own but belong to his fellow servants.[42]

Statements like these got him into trouble with the empress in Constantinople and with a clique of wealthy and powerful people there, and ultimately cost him his life. But the church recognized that John's preaching reflected the heart of Christianity and the gospel. Nothing could be more radical in the ears of those who felt they had too much treasure and property to lose. But nothing could be more normative in the ears of those who took seriously the call of Christ to "deny themselves and take up their cross and follow me" (Mark 8:34).

Speaking with One Voice

The surprising lesson about money and Christians, expounded again and again by leaders from the first five centuries of Christian history, is that for the Christian, all money is God's money. Today, we debate a lot about offerings and tithes and stewardship, whether a Christian is obligated or not to give to the church, and if so, how much. But for the first 500 years of the church, people were practising this, not just talking about it. We have a lot to learn from the words and example of these early brothers and sisters in Christ.

It wasn't just about all money being God's money. It's that our whole lives belong to God. As modern Christians influenced by the West (including by Western missionaries), we often put money in its own special category. But the leaders of the early Christians did not isolate different components like stewardship or discipleship or one's prayer life or participation in the life of a church, as if one could do one and not the others. Just as without prayer, one could question whether one was genuinely a Christian, without stewardship we should ask the same question. A Christian, a follower of Jesus, by definition will be a steward of all the things God has entrusted to her or him.[43] Where this is not happening, it is reasonable to suspect that something is defective in one's Christian life. A good tree will produce good fruit.

That is why in church history again and again the record shows men and women converting to Christianity, and then choosing to give away all of their possessions to the poor before moving into the wilderness or into a monastery in order to pray and become more like Christ. We see example after example of other Christians generously sharing what they have so that the number of poor in their community was drastically reduced – so much so that it drew the mocking attention of the pagan elite, who cared nothing about such things. These Christians did not view the gospel teachings on money and stewardship as mere words. They took Jesus's commands about stewardship seriously. They believed that Christ's love obligated them to love one another even as he had loved them.

> Christ's love obligated them to love one another even as he had loved them.

That doesn't mean that all Christians were exemplary in the use of their resources, or that there weren't examples of rich Christians who tried to have it both ways, with one foot in the world of privilege and the other in the Kingdom of God. The fact that there are sermons and treatises that have survived from this time period indicates that preachers, writers, and leaders saw stewardship as a major ongoing issue they always needed to address. They called each new generation of Christians back to the same criterion of godliness regarding money and property: *Our very lives belong to God, and our calling as Christians is to make what he has given to us available for his use.*

How the church in centuries past understood their call to be stewards of their money and resources – the little that they had – made a tangible difference in the lives of their members and those around them. People around them took notice, and the church kept growing. When we follow their example, perhaps we too will make a similar difference in our world today.

PART THREE

How Stewardship Actually Works

CHAPTER EIGHT

Leading by Example

Transforming stewardship in the church starts not with a programme or a set of official policies, but with you and me. We may not realize it, but we are already teaching and leading people now. People are already noticing how we choose to live and what we choose to do with our money and other resources. It is worth asking, what might my church or my friends learn from looking at my life?

If, for example, I am doing nothing more than everybody else around me, people will notice and take comfort that I am just like them, and that their own lack of stewardship is simply a matter of personal preference. But if I decide to live by a different model, people will notice. My example will challenge some, threaten others, and motivate still others.

If I decide to live by a different model, people will notice.

What has to change in our churches are the hearts of the men, women, and young people who attend. And programmes cannot affect that sort of change. This is why setting an example for others to follow is crucial. When you start to live the reality of discipleship and stewardship, people will soon realize that your example has far more power than your words will ever have.

The Way Stewardship Works: Resurrection Life

The Bible provides several powerful metaphors for what needs to happen in our individual hearts if God's way of stewardship is to take root. The first is *new life in Christ*. What does that actually mean?

The apostle Paul writes in 2 Corinthians 5:14 that: "the love of Christ urges us on, because we are convinced that one has died for all; therefore all have died" (NRSV-A). He is saying that in a spiritual way that reflects reality from God's perspective, we become partakers in Christ's death. Because Christ became human like us and even participated in a human death, he is able in turn to invite us to participate in his resurrected life.

But Christ did not do all this in order for us to simply keep on living as before. No, says Paul. Instead, "he died for all, so that those who live might live no longer for themselves, but for him who died and was raised for them" (2 Corinthians 5:15). The metaphor that Paul is applying to our lives as Christians is that we die with Christ, who died on account of our sin and rebellion. When we are raised with Christ to new life, we do not go back to our old ways of living, our old priorities, our old selfish habits and sins. That old life is *dead*. Our new life is Christ's. We live no longer for ourselves. We live for Christ.

As Paul says at the end of this 2 Corinthians passage: "If anyone is in Christ, there is a new creation: everything old has passed away; see, everything has become new!" (2 Corinthians 5:17). It is this transformation brought about by our new life in Christ that makes possible the Christian life we read about in the Gospels and the rest of the New Testament. Made alive in Christ, made alive to Christ, we can now lay aside our agendas and follow him. Our lives are no longer our own but Christ's. That means our time is Christ's. Our skills are Christ's. Our money is Christ's. Our opportunities are Christ's. Our marriages and relationships are Christ's. Our possessions are Christ's. Christianity is no longer just a religious thing we do on Sundays. Because Christ has made us alive in him, everything is about him. Everything is his.

I acknowledge that this is an expensive call. It can't be sugar-coated. This totally surrendered version of Christianity is not one among many options we can choose. It is the only Christianity assumed by the New Testament. The Lord is asking everything of us, just as he told the rich young ruler: "Sell all that you own and distribute the money to the poor, and you will have treasure in heaven; then come follow me" (Luke 18:22). That young man went away sad, because Jesus asked of him *everything*.

We might prefer an easy path to heaven, thinking salvation is like an insurance policy to save us from the fires of hell while we keep doing what we want to do. But this is not the salvation we read about in the Gospels. Whenever the salvation of Christ touches a person's heart, there we find transformation – new creation! Think about what happened to Zacchaeus the tax collector, or the Gadarene demoniac, or Saul of Tarsus. Grace does not leave a life unchanged.

We say with Paul in his letter to the church in Galatia: "I have been crucified with Christ; and it is no longer I who live, but it is Christ who lives in me. And the life I now live in the flesh I live by faith in the Son of God, who loved me and gave himself for me" (Galatians 2:19b-20). This is the most important step with respect to stewardship. It's the most important step with regard to anything Christian. If we learn this, if we *do* this, everything else will follow.

Laying It on the Altar

The second Bible metaphor that helps us better understand what stewardship means is the Old Testament picture of *sacrifice*. You will remember that as part of the covenant God made with Israel at Mount Sinai, the people of Israel were to celebrate three special feasts every year: the feast of unleavened bread (Pascha), the feast of the first-fruits, and the feast of the ingathering of the full harvest. What made these feasts unusual was that they were not to be celebrated at home. Instead, everyone who was able to travel was to travel to the special place of worship – the Tabernacle or, later, the Temple in Jerusalem. Everyone was to bring what they were going to need for the journey there and back, as well as for the week or so they would spend in Jerusalem. This included everything they would need for worship.

Moses records the Lord's words:

> Three times a year all your males shall appear before the Lord your God at the place that he will choose: at the festival of unleavened bread, at the festival of weeks, and at the festival of booths. They shall not appear before the Lord empty-handed; all shall give as they are able, according to the blessing of the Lord your God that he has given you (Deuteronomy 16:16-17).

Notice that these festivals involved physically reorienting oneself around the Lord and his covenant. But going – being physically present – was not enough. Each man brought with him an offering for the Lord, usually in the form of livestock – sheep, goats, cattle. This meant choosing from one's animals those that would be taken to the festival. (In later years, one's sheep or goats or cows could be sold in the local market and the money taken to Jerusalem in order to buy the equivalent offering there. One of the reasons Jesus drove out the money changers from the court of the Gentiles at the Jerusalem Temple may have been that the sellers of animals for sacrifice were taking advantage of the poor by charging exorbitant prices.)

Sacrifice was central to Old Covenant worship, not just because of the act itself, but because of what sacrifice demonstrated about the individual worshipper. The act of sacrifice was a complex picture of giving to the Lord a portion of what was God's already. God had a claim, not just on one sheep but on the entire flock. He had a claim, not just on one bag of grain, but on the whole harvest. Why? Because the source of everything is God. We make the sacrifice not because God needs the offering.

> Sacrifice was meant to remind the worshipper that all that the person owned had come from God.

Rather the sacrifice represents us – we are the ones on the altar giving ourselves to God. So sacrifice was meant to remind the worshipper that all that the person owned had come from God.

The second thing about sacrifice is that the offering was taken away from some common use and given over to a new and different use. Depending on the sacrifice and the purpose, grain might be offered by sprinkling it on the altar fire, or a token consumed by fire and the rest put aside for the holy use of feeding the priests. A lamb would be taken from the common use of the family's flock and given to the Lord. At the Tabernacle or Temple, it would be slaughtered, its blood splashed against the altar's side, and then either burned whole, or in part while the rest was consumed as part of the holy food for the priests. In both cases of grain or lamb (or of any of the other mandated sacrifices), the offered sacrifice now belonged exclusively to the Lord, to be used as the Lord intended.

The New Testament writers understood from the start that Jesus's own sacrifice of himself on the cross fulfilled the whole purpose for the Old Covenant sacrificial system and accomplished what all the many sacrifices could never do, which was to deal with sin at its source. Sacrifices are no longer needed from us to atone for our sins with the blood of animals. They were never sufficient anyway. But the apostle Paul, for example, still finds the idea of sacrifice as a useful way to describe our own response to the grace of God and the love of Christ.

> I appeal to you therefore, brothers and sisters, by the mercies of God, that you present your bodies as a living sacrifice, holy and acceptable to God, which is your spiritual worship. Do not be conformed to this world, but be transformed by the renewing of your minds, so that you may discern what is the will of God – what is good and acceptable and perfect (Romans 12:1-2).

The difference between Old Covenant worship and Christian worship is that in the past, the worshipper offered part of his flock or crops for God to use. Now that we Christians have been bought out of our slavery to sin and death, now that we are twice-owned by God (once by creation and now by redemption), our worship is not to offer a *part* of what we have or who we are. Our worship is to offer it *all*. We place *ourselves* on the altar. Paul does not think this is extreme; he calls this our "reasonable" service (or worship). As God's offering, you and I no longer belong to ourselves. All we have, all we are, all we own – *everything* is placed on the altar for God to use as he desires.

I admit, this is not what we usually experience in our various services on Sunday morning. Many of us are just doing our religious duty, offering our token bits, and then going about our lives once we get home without truly grasping the gospel or its implications for our lives.

If this is true, we may have wandered far from what God is calling us to be and do as his people. But God hasn't left us without a way to escape our self-constructed personal religions of compromise. He has constructed a narrow path back to his call for us to be his disciples and stewards. The Lord Jesus was willing to work with his twelve disciples over the course of three years. That should give us all hope. It is a journey – *his* journey – that he calls us on.

Here are suggestions for beginning to experience the transformation and change that Jesus makes possible in our own lives and churches.

Practical Ways to Lead People by Example into Stewardship and Discipleship

1. Make a decision to follow Christ wherever he leads.

Many people make a decision for Christ, trust Christ as their personal Saviour, and claim to have been born again. But some of these same people are still very much in charge of their lives. Perhaps nobody has ever taught them what stewardship and discipleship are all about.

Whatever the reason for their lack, real Christianity starts with full surrender. The reason so many churches are weak, self-consumed, divided by conflict, and always short of funds is because the Christians and even the leaders have never surrendered their agenda to Christ. They have not grasped that resurrection life is a life lived no longer for ourselves but for Christ who loved us. They have not realized that real worship means laying everything we are and have on the altar, so that now it is God's to use for his purpose and glory.

It is easy to sing "I have decided to follow Jesus", but few of us realize the cost it involves. According to multiple online sources, these were the last words of a Christian martyr in India, who refused to deny Christ when the village chief threatened him with death, then killed both his children and his wife before him, finally killing him too. This gives a whole new weight to his words: "Though none go with me, still I will follow. The world behind me, the cross before me."

Full surrender is the step that Peter, Andrew, James, and John took by the Lake in Galilee when Jesus called them to follow him. It's the same step the apostle Paul took when he was struck off his horse by a vision of Christ as he approached Damascus. It's the same step Anthony of Egypt took after he inherited his wealthy parents' estate upon their death. Anthony could have chosen the comfortable life his parents left for him or tried to make some other compromise. Instead, after making allowance for his sister, he gave away everything he had to the poor and followed Christ into the wilderness. We think of St Anthony as the Father of Monasticism 1800 years later, but at the time, the young Coptic Christian was simply trying to say yes to Jesus.

2. Conduct a fearless inventory of your life.

By saying "conduct a fearless inventory of your life", I am borrowing the language from the fourth step of Alcoholics Anonymous's 12-step programme that has been so useful in helping addicted men and women. Once we hand ourselves over to the Lord, we need to be honest with ourselves. What choices are we making that are not in line with the Lord's priorities? How have we contributed to brokenness in our relationships with those around us? How do our actions reflect a life that is self-centred and not God-centred?

Exploring these questions may take us down a long and winding path, but we will begin to see just how far we have wandered from the Lord. We may realize we are like the prodigal son, who found himself hungry and out of resources, eating pigs' food to keep himself alive. Jesus says he suddenly came to his senses and said, "How many of my father's hired hands have bread enough and to spare, but here I am dying of hunger!" (Luke 15:17). And so the young man started his journey back to his father's house.

So it is with you and me. At some point, you and I must come to our senses and realize where we are and where we belong instead. When this happens, we will begin our own journey back to our Father's house. But it won't happen unless we have the courage to ask ourselves some hard questions.

3. Make a personal record that reflects how you actually spend your money.

To help us understand what we are doing with our resources, it really helps to lay out the actual numbers in front of us. Figuring out where our resources are going shows us precisely where our heart is. Jesus himself says: "Where your treasure is, there your heart will be also" (Matthew 6:21).

We may have a general idea of what we are doing with our money. But people are often surprised when they sit down and actually follow the money.

> People are often surprised when they sit down and actually follow the money.

To do this, purchase a small notebook. Start with the first day of the month. On the left-hand side, record the date, amount, and source of everything that comes into your possession, whether it is your salary, your spouse's salary, gifts, or payment in kind (if you are given a chicken, give the monetary amount it represents). On the right-hand side, begin a list of everything you spend. This means writing down the amount spent at the market for onions and tomatoes, the amount you paid to the power company for electricity, the amount paid to your house help or your babysitter. If you put money away in a savings account or are paying a loan, include that. Include the amount you contribute at church and any support you give to other people or groups. Record it all. This will take discipline, but the knowledge you gain will be well worth the effort.

Try to order your account according to categories, such as food, school fees, transportation, or entertainment. Make your categories useful to you and your situation. At the end of the month you can add up your expenses, taking note of what percentage of your income went for what. I started doing this more than thirty years ago and have found it so useful that I am still doing it today.

Date	Income Amount	Source	Expense Amount	Description	Category

When we know what we are spending our resources on, then we will be in a position to know what our next step should be. But we have to start with good data.

4. Ask yourself, "What does the way I spend money tell me about my priorities?"

Most of us will be shocked with how much we are spending on things of no eternal value, and how little we are giving to facilitate God's kingdom. What this information helps us do is to be intentional about how we are using our money, and more importantly, intentional about putting our resources into those things that are important to God. This is where Jesus's words to his disciples – that they should not worry about what they will eat or how they will be clothed – come home. Instead, we are to "seek first [God's] kingdom and his righteousness, and all these things will be given to [us] as well" (Matthew 6:33 NIV).

5. Adjust your giving.

It is true that people who are poor have little cash to contribute. But we are not all as poor as we think we are. Many of us have jobs, or raise crops, or have chickens and cattle. We cannot claim we have *nothing* to give the Lord and his priorities.

Much of the time, there are other reasons suppressing our giving. Maybe there is no transparency in what the church is doing with the offerings it collects. Maybe there is little if any vision of what the church should do and be in the community. Maybe it's just a matter of habit or laziness – *the church doesn't need me to give, so why bother?*

But for the church to be the community of God's people in its local place, it needs its people to make that possible. And we need to ensure that there is accountability (more on this to come). After all, the church is not *them*, it's *us*. We ourselves are part of the church body, not just the people we criticize. So we give to help facilitate the Kingdom of God in this place. We give because we are the ones whom God is using to make his kingdom possible.

Stewardship and discipleship are not church programmes, they are aspects of our individual relationship with the Lord. If we are in relationship with Christ, we will be growing as disciples and stewards. This is the good tree that bears good fruit that Jesus talks about (Matthew 7:17-18). The tree that bears no fruit or bad fruit is the life that knows nothing of a relationship with Christ. The key is to know Christ, to learn from Christ, to be filled with Christ, and to respond accordingly.

6. Don't just talk and discuss. Do something!

We Christian leaders are good at talking about what we *could* be doing, or even talking about what *those* people should be doing, but often not so good about actually doing it ourselves. One way to get people involved in ministry is to create an opportunity to help others outside the church (and within as well). I am aware of one church that had a handful of men who were skilled carpenters, plumbers, and electricians, as well as other men and women who didn't necessarily have those skills but were willing to learn. This group would learn about someone who had major structural issues in their house and would make arrangements to come on a Saturday and begin the repairs. Working on one house at a time, they would do what they could and call for outside help if they needed it.

Because of their reputation, the church began receiving requests from people not associated with the church, or with any church, so there was never any shortage of opportunity. The group would commit to one Saturday a month and then do what needed to be done over the next several weeks. There are now new families attending the church as a direct result of the work of these men and women.

The point of this is to do something, almost anything, in the name of Christ that gets Christians using their time and talents and resources to help other people. This is part of what it means to be Christ's disciple, and for the church to be the body of Christ, the presence of Jesus in the world. It not only reflects the hearts of those participating, but it is also God's means of blessing people both in and beyond the church.

When we realize that our entire lives belong to God, it is only reasonable for him to direct us in how we use everything that he has given us. When we see our lives this way, we become real stewards. We see that our calling from God is to manage what he has given us for his glory.

As we begin to take an inventory of our possessions, surrender ourselves to God, and realign our budgets with God's priorities, we will often rediscover a joy we didn't know we could experience. We have been freed from the grip of money to live fully for our Master, Jesus Christ. The Holy Spirit begins to change our hearts as we follow Christ with our finances. Our example will often inspire others to do the same. When we give up things that the world values, we make a statement that there is something worth it – something of much greater value that we stand to gain.

> It is only reasonable for [God] to direct us in how we use everything that he has given us.

CHAPTER NINE

Building Trust and Integrity

A married couple I know (I'll call them Mary and Cyrus) started attending a small but growing church in their city. Friends had talked about this church and how the pastor almost never talked about money or offerings except when preaching on a passage that dealt with financial issues. The church programmes, such as Sunday school, seemed to have no problem recruiting volunteers to lead them. And people were generous in their giving.

After a few weeks Mary and Cyrus began to understand why. At the end of the month, the church board posted a detailed accounting of how much had been received each week in the offerings and what had been done with it. This monthly posting was placed next to a copy of the annual church budget, which had been voted on by the entire membership. After all, by approving the church budget (and the ministry priorities it represented) for the year, the membership had also agreed to do their part to make the plan a reality.

After some months getting to know the leadership and other members, Mary and Cyrus decided this was a fellowship they wanted to join. The church ministry priorities were things they could enthusiastically support. They liked the transparency and accountability very much.

And they liked that the church, both leaders and members, were committed to both evangelism and missions. The church, in fact, was supporting two missionary families working in different unreached parts of the country. The church also had a plan to start new congregations from its own membership, rather than simply trying to be a big church.

The couple felt they could start giving and not wonder what was actually happening with their money. They were excited to become part of a community that was committed to something more than just serving itself. Both of them, having good jobs were in a position to support the church generously. And they did.

Winning People's Trust

If people trust their money is going where their leaders claim it is going, they are more likely to give. Mary and Cyrus's experience shows just how powerful a fundamental commitment to good management and accountability can be in the life of a congregation. The opposite – a lack of transparency, misappropriation of funds, and outright stealing (embezzlement) by church leaders – will kill stewardship and trust, resulting eventually in the ugly death of the church.

This chapter shows pastors and church leaders how to be good stewards of the money and resources God provides through the generosity of his people. These principles can apply to local churches, Christian organizations, denominational offices, schools, and programmes. All of these benefit from careful management and accountability.

We will also consider the big-picture issues that are critical to the success or failure of giving and stewardship. We will ask whether we are in line with what God is calling us to be and do as his people in the world, and whether we have a vision compelling enough to draw people toward God's mission for us.

I know from personal experience that many Christians want to do the right thing and give to God's work. However, they see what is going on and are weary of dysfunctional and self-serving leadership in their church. It's this majority of African Christians who, if better informed, would be empowered to lead the church into better stewardship and discipleship. These men and women who are serious about living for Christ are in a position to respond to a clear vision and mission to be the church God is calling them to be. To help these leaders and concerned church members take the next step, we now take a closer look at stewardship in the church.

Good Church Stewardship – So Easy, So Challenging

Good church stewardship means managing the funds and resources entrusted by the members to their leaders in a way that glorifies God by furthering the church's mission and enabling its vision to become a reality. This includes not only the funds that are given through church offerings but also the use of facility and properties, and the use of the members' time, property, and spiritual gifts as well.

Church giving is not an automatic thing, nor should it be. Too many church leaders assume that if they take a collection, people should give "as unto the Lord". But many factors are at play with respect to whether a member of a particular congregation should support that church's ministry or not. Too many of us have learned the hard way that just because someone claims to be a Christian leader, a pastor, a bishop, or an evangelist, doesn't mean that person can be trusted with our money, or that they have the Lord's interests in mind. From personal experience, I know that many African Christians are generous with what they have, freely lending to family and community members. So where little is being given in the church offering Sunday by Sunday, there is usually a reason for it.

Wise leaders will recognize instantly that trust cannot be assumed; it must be earned. Just as many of us have learned the hard way not to give our hard-earned money to random people who come up to us with a story of need, so we have learned to be similarly cautious with our resources at church. Too many of us have had unhappy experiences with the way money has been used and abused in the churches we attend.

Financial accountability is one of several indicators of a congregation's overall spiritual health. Another indicator is whether the leaders and members have a clear grasp of the gospel and understand what our response as disciples should be. And yet another indicator of a local church's spiritual health is the presence (or absence) of a worthy mission that takes the church outside of itself and propels it into the world through charity, evangelism, and missions.

> Indicators of a healthy church include financial accountability, a clear grasp of the gospel, and outward mission.

I could list others, but each of these three is a crucial aspect of stewardship. The degree to which they are present or absent in the life of a congregation is a good indication of a church's overall health.

Power and Control

One of the major reasons today why people get so upset over a church's finances is because control over the money has become the major way the pastor, priest, or leader exercises control over the church. If the leader controls the money, then anybody in the church who needs anything must come to him or her. This, of course, can lead to volcanic conflicts between staff members, between the board and the pastor, and among the congregation.

Of course, this is the way many of us have experienced leadership in organizations, be it political, business, or religious. Controlling the money means controlling access to resources for yourself and for everyone else. Getting control of those resources puts one in a position to help both oneself and one's friends. This, sadly, is the definition of success in too many places on our continent.

As long as controlling the money is the dominant goal of leadership in a church, any kind of real Christianity and any experience of New Testament priorities and mission simply withers away. Leaders who control the church in this way may succeed in building a top-down business model, developing a powerful network of relationships based on patronage. But they have taken their church far from what Jesus and the apostles called the church and its mission to be.

For example, I am aware of a certain bishop who took over the finance office. Since he now decides which clergy and employees get paid what salary and when, the bishop is assured that nobody will disagree with him, lest they suffer the consequences. One could argue that the bishop is simply being a patron to the rest of the church. However, the bishop is using intimidation, implied threats and fear to make sure everybody does what he wants them to do.

Recovering the New Testament identity and mission of one's church is the only way out of the power-and-control trap. The church and its leadership must decide that Christ's mission for the church is bigger than any leader, and that leaders serve Christ and his mission, rather than the other way around. This may be troublesome for our church leaders in Africa, but it was just as challenging for Peter, Andrew, James, John, and the rest of the disciples (Mark 10:35-45).

Jesus has a mission for his church, and it is our job as leaders to understand what that mission is and then make it happen. Stewardship, as we have described in the preceding chapters, will not happen unless we can say with truthfulness, "Your kingdom come. Your will be done, on earth as it is in heaven" (Matthew 6:10 NRSV-A). Bringing you and me and our church to the point of saying that, and meaning it, is what discipleship is all about.

Christian Organizations and Stewardship

In Christian organizations, it is the role of the board of directors to ensure accountability for finances and the organization's stated mission and goals. It is the role of the executive (leader) to implement the board's direction. It is the responsibility of the board to ensure that the budget is being followed and that all of the money can be accounted for.

Too often in Christian institutions – whether they are schools, clinics, ministries, or orphanages – the board doesn't exist or isn't involved. An appointment to a board is primarily an honour, because the board exists only on paper. I was asked to serve on the board of a church-sponsored school in Kenya, but over the next several years, I was never contacted to attend board meetings.

Whenever I discover that there is no functioning board of directors for some Christian school, seminary, hospital, or orphanage, I have learned to expect the worst. That institution is usually being run for the benefit of the director. Even if the director is not personally misappropriating funds, the institution is likely being run in such a way that would make accountability awkward for the director.

Some boards try to do too much – specifically trying to manage the institution, when that is the reason they have a director. It's the director's job to manage the institution; it's the board's job to oversee the director, to support the director, and to ensure that he or she has what is needed to do the job. The board also holds the director accountable to perform the job according to the job description and to follow the institution's policies and direction according to the constitution. But when there is a director trying to manage the organization, and the board is also trying to manage the organization by interfering with the work of the director, it will not go well for anyone. In the resulting conflict the organization and its work will suffer.

This is not unlike a church, where there is a pastor or priest responsible for leading the church in worship and ministry. The purpose of the church board is not to do the pastor's job. Rather the church board oversees and supports the pastor and other staff members as they provide leadership for the rest of the members. The board makes sure the pastor is paid a wage that he or she can live on, and that the pastor has what is needed to fulfil the ministry. The board is also responsible for the church's finances.

To protect a pastor from any suspicion of impropriety or temptation, a pastor should never have anything to do with money collected from the members. Offerings are given to a church, not to the pastor. The pastor is paid out of the money given to the church. It is the church board's responsibility to ensure that the money is handled in a transparent way and that proper records are kept, so anyone with any concerns about how the church's money is being spent can easily get answers.

These structures of accountability do not grow in an empty field. Land needs to be cultivated, the seeds sown, the young sprouts nurtured, and the weeds chopped down. It is the same process when changing the institutional culture of an organization or a church. The governance must be restructured. A proper constitution needs to be written and then followed. This means appointing a board of directors or governors whose responsibility is to approve the vision and budget, oversee the director, ensure that the resources are being used properly, and check that the desired outcomes are being achieved. It is a straightforward process, but it takes effort and, most of all, willingness to make it happen. Depending on the institution, it may require a revolution in the way the institution has always done things.

The benefits of choosing accountability and embracing stewardship are profound. One of the most exciting board transformations I have seen was at a school whose board micromanaged everything about the school's affairs. Someone taught the board members about alternative models of board governance, and they realized the difference between their role and the role of the director. The director and the teachers were freed to focus on what they were hired and gifted to do, and the school became much more functional and effective as a result.

These basic procedures for both institutions and churches, when put in place, will inspire trust among the church's members and the institution's stakeholders. Trust is the mother of blessing in any ministry or organization. So when these procedures are not in place and trust has not been maintained, our institutions can expect trouble, as many of us know from sad experience.

Big ships travelling the oceans teach us something of how difficult it is to change organizations. We like to think that change can happen instantaneously, that all we need to do is to set a clear course, or to get everyone to repent and decide to follow Jesus, and then we're done. But experience teaches something else. The captain of a big ship on the high seas may realize the ship is heading in the wrong direction. He may then give the order to turn. But it takes a long time and many kilometres for a big ship to change directions.

The same is true with our lives, our churches, and our organizations. Change only happens instantly in our dreams or on television. We may decide we want to change. But it takes time, sometimes a lot of time, to bring the rest of our lives around in line with what our minds want to do. It takes time to bring everyone else in the church along with us if we want to make a change. Patience is one of the fruits of the Spirit's work in our lives for a reason.

And Then There's Corruption

A further reason that many church members refuse to give generously to their churches is the corrupt way those offerings are used by leaders. If I suspect that my pastor or priest or an elder is pocketing what is given to the Lord, I will not be a very cheerful giver the next Sunday. Corruption in the church – or in any Christian organization – is stealing from God, pure and simple. Corrupt leaders divert money from its intended purpose of enabling ministry to instead enrich themselves. They raise funds from church members or donors for one project and then divert those funds into something entirely different. This only suppresses future giving, as church members choose to take the money they have set aside for the Lord and give it to other causes.

A growing Christian school needed two new dormitories, one for young men and the other for young women. Land had already been bought. The denominational leader decided to hold a fundraiser. Many people, including politicians (it was an election year), were invited. The committee in charge set a goal and organized the event after church services in one of the bigger congregations. Ministers from all over attended. And the politicians did as well.

The fundraiser was a smashing success. The contributions were more than double what the committee had hoped. Everybody went home happy.

Time passed, but nothing happened. There were no construction crews digging foundations, no truckloads of building supplies. Just an overgrown field. Later it emerged that funding had suddenly appeared to construct a beautiful church in a different part of the country. There were rumours about what happened to all the money raised for the dormitories, but nothing was ever admitted. All that people knew was that the money they had contributed to build dormitories had disappeared. The empty, overgrown field is there to this day.

Churches operate on trust, and when that trust is broken, churches break down as well. Some people actually go into Christian ministry for the same reason other people go into politics: it gives them access to resources. Access then leads to compromise. The more times people compromise and choose to take money for themselves that doesn't belong to them, the more they become corrupt. Corruption can kill the institution as well as entangle the corrupt person in an ever-increasing tangle of lies, threats, and abuse of authority.

Such people become little more than parasites, living off the stolen monies and properties of other hardworking, well-intentioned people. Corruption in the church is like thousands of ticks on a cape buffalo. At the very least, corrupt leaders cause the church to become spiritually weak, unable to take on those tasks of evangelism and missions in the community that healthy churches normally do. In some cases, corruption can even kill the church.

> Corrupt men and women leave a bad smell that drives people away from the church.

God calls a church into existence in a particular place so that the gathered Christians can become the presence and love of Christ in that community. But corruption robs God of his church and frustrates God's purpose and mission for his people. Just as something dead by the side of the road begins to have a bad smell unless it is taken away and buried, corrupt men and women leave a bad smell that drives people away from the church.

Here are symptoms to look for if you suspect the church's finances are being mismanaged:

- First, there will be no transparency. No reports of church giving will be published. No accounting of church spending will be produced.
- No receipts will be given.
- No audits of the church's books will ever be undertaken.
- Offerings will be counted in private, with no oversight.

When these things are true, it doesn't automatically mean that someone is stealing church money. It could just mean that the leadership is managing the church's property and accounts unprofessionally. But it could also mean that someone has set up procedures to prevent anyone from holding them to account for how the church's money is being mismanaged, misappropriated, or stolen.

If you suspect that the leadership is corrupt, you will need evidence that proves the case. This is difficult, especially if the culture is based on an honour-shame dichotomy and is averse to direct confrontation. In some cases, there may be a respected leader or congregant, who may be seen as a peer or elder to the leader in question. Confiding in them may be an appropriate first step, so they can bring up the issue to the leader. The leaders in question should be given the opportunity to present their side of the story. If the problem persists, you may need to have that conversation as part of a group of concerned church members, which shows that you are not the only one concerned.

Unfortunately, if corrupt people don't want to change or take responsibility for their behaviour, there is not much one can do to help them. If the evidence is compelling and there is no repentance, the leader should be removed from office. I know of one associate pastor who was brought before the church board and fired because of corruption. I congratulate the church for their godly action. Corrupt leaders who are allowed to remain in place will continue to destroy any church or organization until it has the courage to rid itself of them. If the leader refuses to go, taking the matter to the local authorities is an option. However, because there may be a similar trust issue with the local authorities, the best solution may be just to shake the dust from your feet and leave the church.

Without a Vision, the People Perish

Mismanagement and corruption are obvious ways that local churches miss out on the fullness of what God has called them to do as God's people. Less obvious, but just as damaging to church stewardship, is when there is not a vision for what the local church is called to be and do. Churches that exist only for themselves become ingrown and stagnant. In time, all such churches choke out genuine spiritual life and are left with a toxic environment that is little different from the surrounding world.

Nature illustrates this point powerfully. Lake Natron on the Tanzania-Kenya border receives water from a few small rivers and streams flowing into it during the rainy seasons. But because the lake lies in a depression that's surrounded by hills all around, no water ever leaves except by evaporation. The result is that over the centuries, the water has become increasingly alkaline and salty. The waters have become toxic, so most of whatever once lived in the lake died long ago. The few fish that live in the lake stay in the less salty parts, where fresh water from one of the rivers enters the lake before it mixes and becomes poisonous. Otherwise, the lake only hosts some bacteria and other microorganisms that enjoy a diet of salt. With its eerie red water from the bacteria, and the flamingos that come to nest in the alkaline shallows, Lake Natron is a hot and deadly place.

Contrast Lake Natron with Lake Victoria to the northwest, the huge freshwater lake surrounded by Uganda, Tanzania and Kenya. Similar to Lake Natron, waters flood into the lake from many streams and rivers, and also from the tropical downpours that rise up almost daily over the lake and its watershed. But the difference is that while Natron has no outlet for its waters and is toxic to almost all forms of life, Lake Victoria's waters flow both in and out. Victoria is drained by the Nile as it begins its long journey to Egypt and the Mediterranean Sea.

Unlike Lake Natron, Lake Victoria not only receives water, but it also gives water. As a result, Victoria's water is fresh, and it supports hundreds of different species of fish, many of which are prized by aquarium hobbyists around the world. Victoria is a living ecosystem, receiving and giving its water in a way that enables it to support an amazing variety of life in its waters and around its shores.

Too many churches are like Lake Natron, spending everything they get on themselves with no thought or vision for what God might have created their church to do. They may have beautiful buildings, like some of the mega-churches in our capital cities. They may attract many wealthy and powerful people. Their leaders may be consulted by government officials. They may have exciting worship and lines of people coming forward for prayer after the service. But instead of these indicators, we should focus on their impact on people's lives, on the surrounding community, on poverty reduction, on job creation, on ministry to the sick or imprisoned. If we don't see an outflow of resources and love, these churches are, to borrow a metaphor from Jesus, whitewashed tombs – beautiful and impressive on the outside, but as dead as Lake Natron on the inside.

By spending everything they get on themselves, they long ago became spiritually stagnant. According to the world and many of their peers, they were successful, with a huge building, a big crowd, and the latest in technology. If you want to be entertained with the latest and the best that popular Christianity has to offer, this church is the place to be. The sad thing is that the leadership has often taken their size or cash flow as a sign of God's blessing on what they were doing. But are they willing to ask the harder, more uncomfortable questions about what *God's* agenda for them might be?

Leaders whose vision for the church is growth for the sake of growth have doomed that church to spiritual irrelevance. Some leaders put their index finger in the air to determine from which way the wind of current trends is blowing. Then they organize their church on the basis of what is popular – new music styles, teaching what people want to hear, or fun activities and events. They may attract a crowd, but they take people on a ride further away from God and his kingdom, not closer. Targeting to simply grow big is a small goal. All these outward signs can be manufactured by human cleverness. One doesn't really need God at all to be this kind of church.

> Popular music styles, fun activities and events may attract a crowd, but they take people on a ride further away from God and his kingdom, not closer.

God Has an Agenda?

God does indeed have an agenda. But too many of our churches have planted themselves on the far margins of God's purpose for his people. Too many of us aren't aware that he's called us to himself, not only because of his great love for us, yes; but also because of his great love for those around us. And God gives us the riches of his grace, the riches of his provision, the riches of reconciled relationships, and the fullness of his Holy Spirit *not* so that we can spend it on ourselves, but so that we might be the means for people around us to experience his love. *We* are part of the answer to that prayer we pray so often: "Your kingdom come. Your will be done, on earth as it is in heaven" (Matthew 6:10). The church is God's Plan A for reaching his lost world. And there is no Plan B.

God's agenda for us as his redeemed men and women is to make us more and more like Christ (Ephesians 4:11-13). This is why the Holy Spirit is given to us. The Holy Spirit changes us from the inside out, making us want to leave behind those sins that hinder us, and instead desire with all our hearts to move towards wholeness and healing.

It's the Holy Spirit who gives us new eyes to see Christ for who he is, and who renews our hearts so that we *want* to respond to his love and call. The Holy Spirit puts within each of us the desire to spend time in God's Word and the corresponding desire to respond to God in prayer. The Holy Spirit gives us the capacity and the desire to repent when we do selfish things that hurt other people or ourselves. And the Holy Spirit shows us ways to love the people around us. We find ourselves increasingly motivated by the love of Christ in what we say and do.

If someone were to watch this transformation take hold in our hearts, they would rightly call it a miracle. This is, in fact, the real and verifiable miracle that the Holy Spirit endeavours to work in each one of us. God is undertaking to do in us and through us what we ourselves could never hope to do. It is for this reason that Jesus can say that one will know the tree by its fruit (Luke 6:43-45). The Holy Spirit's work within us will bear good fruit, fruit that ordinary people living their lives in the world around us will never produce on their own (Galatians 5:22-25). And the fruit of the Holy Spirit that our lives produce identifies us as belonging to Jesus. Indeed, we start doing the very things that he would do.

If it is God's agenda to make you and me more like Jesus, it should surprise no one that God's agenda for the local church is to make us the very presence of Jesus in our community. That is why the church is called the body of Christ (1 Corinthians 12:27).

Worship – our response to God – is certainly important, and it is something that Christians both individually and corporately will do. But worship is not the mission or the agenda that God gives to his people.

In some traditions, celebrating the sacraments is central to what the church is meant to do. Of course, the sacraments are vitally important to God's people, being the way God strengthens his people for his mission. But the sacraments are not the mission; they are but a way God uses to strengthen his people for that mission.

And yes, God's people are meant to pray. Prayer is how we bring God into the issues of our hearts, and how God brings us into the issues of *his* heart. Prayer is foundational to the church and to its mission. But prayer is not the mission.

The same can be said about spiritual gifts. They are wonderful channels for building up the body of Christ (see 1 Corinthians 12:14), but they are not the mission of the church: becoming the presence of Christ and bringing his kingdom here on earth as it is in heaven.

Once again, we find ourselves at the very heart of stewardship. As Christians saved from the world and called to be part of God's expanding kingdom, we come with nothing in our hands. Even the abilities and talents we have and the worldly possessions we have accumulated are God's provision and gifts for us. The reason we have been given these things is not so that we can sit on them and then use what we have to judge the relative worth of those around us, nor is it for us to take the higher positions or the seat at the head table. It is not so we can get access to even more possessions or power or perks. Instead, we are to give all that we have and all that we are back to God by serving the people around us. Using what we have in this way is what it means to glorify God.

God is making us his church into the presence of Jesus, not just in our fellowship, but in our neighbourhoods and in our city. As a result, we understand more clearly God's mission and his agenda for his church. We also see how stewardship is meant to work in the local church. The church is empowered by the Holy Spirit to be Jesus in the local community, and all that entails. And the Holy

Spirit equips and empowers his people to do it. We respond to the call and step out in faith, giving ourselves in love to the people around us, just as Jesus did.

As this happens, our church priorities and our church budget will reflect what our mission is. As people begin to see the power of Jesus's love at work in their own lives and in the lives of those they touch in Jesus's name, it feeds back into the worship of the church, because now we as a church have something to thank God for. As we interact with the needs around us, we realize we also have a profound need for God's grace and help, and so our prayers as a church take on a new urgency. These are the things that can happen when we members of a local church know God and are committed to his mission and respond with who we are and what we have. This is the circle of true biblical stewardship.

So Let's Summarize

There are many practical things that churches or Christian organizations can do to remove barriers to good stewardship and to promote healthy finances. Common-sense practices include:
- involving the congregation in preparing and approving an annual budget,
- maintaining transparency in how much money is collected and how it is spent,
- systematically identifying and removing the dark corners of the institution where corruption can take root and grow, and
- having zero tolerance at every level of leadership when integrity is not maintained.

These are all important supports towards establishing and maintaining institutional integrity, so that members and friends can feel confident that the money they are giving to the Lord will be handled responsibly and will go to support the ministry priorities agreed on by all the parties.

But as important as these financial and leadership accountability steps are, they will accomplish nothing on their own unless the church's spiritual house is in order. The three components of a healthy church we have just discussed must be in place if a congregation is to be true to its calling to be the presence of Christ where it has been planted:

- discipleship: total surrender to follow Jesus,
- stewardship: treating all I am and all I have as Christ's, and putting it all at his disposal,
- mission: the body of Christ Jesus loving and serving and bringing his reign on earth.

Take any one of these away, and the church simply cannot function as God's blessing to its members, to the community where they live, or to the wider world with whom they are called to engage in the name of Christ.

But when the church is full of men and women who are committed to follow Christ and grow in his grace, who understand that everything that they have is a gift from God, who steward this blessing for God's agenda and God's glory, who understand the mission God has called them to as a church – then we begin to see the good fruit that Jesus was always so keen to produce in his people.

CHAPTER TEN

What Local Church Stewardship Looks Like

It pleases me to see a growing number of local congregations in Kenya and other African locales that have begun to understand what the Bible teaches about stewardship and money. Their understanding has transformed both their life as a Christian community and their efforts to reach beyond their doors.

It is exciting to be a part of such a local church. Worship services are crowded. People are eager to learn more, so they go to classes or home Bible study and prayer groups. Lots of children come to Sunday school. The youth group is a fun and contagious draw for young people, even from outside the church.

But the most exciting thing is that the members feel they are a part of something bigger. They have clearly understood that being a Christian is more than just attending services; it involves a change in life goals and life direction. It involves a change in priorities, from those that were self-centred to new ones that are God-centred.

It involves a new understanding of one's possessions and salary, indeed of everything one has. No longer do I assume that what is mine is mine, and God gets only what's left over, if anything. Instead, I understand that what is mine has actually been given to me by God, who holds me responsible to use it for his glory. I am now a steward in charge of wisely spending the King's resources on the King's business and the King's priorities.

> No longer do I assume that what is mine is mine, and God gets only what's left over, if anything.

Of course, part of that is the responsible care of my family or my personal needs. But even this is an aspect of my stewardship. God gives me and my family what we need so we can then devote ourselves to what Christ is calling us to do and be as his disciples.

When the local church gets stewardship and money right, the transformation is electrifying. The church becomes the *church*. People start to *care* – which means people start to *love*. Which means people start to *give* – their money, their time, their abilities.

The caring, loving, and giving are contagious. When we see the powerful impact of one person's generosity, we see that we can do the same thing and have a similar impact. It spreads through the entire congregation. We change from demanding our rights and privileges to looking for ways to love, share, and give. We change from being too proud to pay attention to anyone beneath us to, like Jesus, not being afraid to wrap a towel around our waists and wash our neighbours' feet. Instead of being stingy at church offering time, we become like the members of the apostolic church, who willingly even sold land and houses so they could enable the church to care for the poor in their midst.

Please understand: I am not saying that if churches understand stewardship, they will be perfect. They are full of human beings, all of whom are still on the way to becoming like Christ. They still have issues. But churches that understand stewardship are more and more outposts of heaven in their local community.

Where God's kingdom is established in any community, the church becomes a hub for God's love to be experienced and shared. We become people who demonstrate to the rest of our neighbours what it means to be made in the image of God, what it means to be forgiven, what it means to be a disciple of our Lord Jesus, and what it means to be filled with the Holy Spirit. We become the beachhead of the Kingdom of God in this world, the point where God's grace begins to invade and take over the rest of the world.

The Kingdom of God is simply the place where God rules, where God is in control. Obviously, this does not mean actual square kilometres of territory. The place where God reigns today is in human hearts. God intends his church to be the place where he reigns. God intends our lives to be the place where he reigns.

What follows are the stories of three churches I know that are dealing with the need for true discipleship and stewardship. Two are making strong progress, while one is not. Their examples are instructive for us all.

A Church under Pressure

This particular church began meeting secretly in a school classroom at a time when a Marxist regime dominated its country and Christians were being persecuted. Because churches in the capital city had been shuttered, it began to attract men and women who were serious about their Christian faith and who were not afraid to suffer if the authorities mounted a crackdown.

The leaders of this church decided from the very beginning to be transparent about finances, as the government had used the pretext of corruption (often sadly true) to close many churches over the years. Meticulous records were kept of offerings, any outside gifts, and how every bit was spent, including receipts.

The congregation continued to grow, even through the tumult of an anti-government insurgency. The church outgrew its classroom and was seeking a place where they could build a proper meeting place. Since an insurrection was growing in the countryside, the government decided to attempt to curry favour with the outside world, showcasing that they were not persecutors of Christians and churches but allowing freedom of worship for Christians. So when the church's leaders approached the newly receptive government ministry with their request for land and permission to build a church, the government eventually approved it.

But the land they were given was actually an old garbage dump, with a stinking river running alongside it. There was a huge tree in the middle of the dump that had for many years hosted traditional religious practices such as sacrifices to ward off curses and attract blessings.

Nevertheless, the church, after prayer, decided to accept the government's offer. Everybody helped in the massive effort to remove the rubbish and reclaim the land.

During this time, open warfare reached the capital. Tank battles erupted on the streets. The church property happened to include a steep hill on one side, and on that hill a government tank took up a position to shell insurgents on the other side of the neighbourhood. When the tank itself was neutralized, it began rolling down the hill, all the way until it crashed into the river.

When the government finally fell, it was replaced by a new government that allowed freedom of religion. Released from fear of persecution, many people flooded into the newly opened churches across the country, including the congregation meeting in the former garbage dump. By this time enough money had been raised to build a beautiful building that could seat 800 people. The sanctuary was surrounded by a courtyard, and in the surrounding buildings was space for a theological college, church offices, and a library.

Being one of the few churches that offered services in English, the church attracted not only local people from all over the capital but also members of the diplomatic community, NGOs, mission personnel, and even government officials. Sunday mornings required two services, which filled the main hall to capacity, with Sunday school for several hundred children in between. To accommodate internationals who did not speak English, additional services were begun in French and Korean.

Through all of this, the church maintained its high standards of accountability. The board hired a business manager and a separate accountant to oversee all of the finances. The church had 14 ministry staff and more than 30 cleaners, gardeners, and security people on its payroll. To meet with government audit regulations, all of the books had to be in order for when the outside auditors came to inspect.

Many people felt they could trust this church and how it dealt with money. The church board regularly published its budget and also published what was given week to week. So members gave generously. For many years, the church had the largest budget and offering of any congregation in the country.

Among the ministries supported by the church was a significant outreach to HIV-AIDS widows and orphans. There was also an active youth ministry, as well as church-supported Bible studies.

There were challenges as well over the years; it was not a perfect community. There were tensions between church elders and the pastors, and conflicts in terms of church priorities and ministries. But the unity of the body always won the day.

If you pass by the compound today, you would never guess that a garbage dump used to be there. The old tank has slowly settled into the riverbed, but the turret and cannon can still be seen to this day. The huge tree, where local diviners used to perform rituals, was struck by lightning several years ago and fell across the parking lot. The old tree was cut up and the wood donated to neighbours.

The church went through many changes from the time it was a small secret classroom meeting to its current beautiful compound, but its stewardship practices remained constant. It always maintained financial transparency and used church funds for ministry to its members and the surrounding community. This church is an amazing example of what a church can become when we align our priorities with Christ's mission for his world.

A Church from the Ground Up

A parish was established twenty years ago between two informal settlements in an African city, and a piece of land was donated by a family. The bishop appointed a priest, and plans were made to hold a fundraiser to raise money for a simple temporary structure. The event was successful, and the families themselves contributed corrugated iron sheets, cement, and wood for the frame. A small structure was built. Several outdoor toilets were dug. A fence was built around the property.

As soon as services began, curious neighbours began attending. News travelled fast, and other Christians who lived nearby but who travelled to more distant churches visited as well. People liked what they experienced, and they stayed. Those who were new to the church were catechized and then baptized, with their wives and children.

As the church grew, it formed a parish board. They began making plans for taking care of their members as well as for reaching out to the community. The parish board challenged members to give sacrificially so that the church could be Christ's body in their community. They made a budget so everyone would know what was needed and how the money would be spent.

They set up a checking account to take care of ongoing needs. They also set up a savings account for future projects they envisioned. One big project was on everyone's minds. Attendance had grown so much that their small building was now getting cramped. Moreover, there was no place to take the children for Sunday school, to prepare tea for after the services, or to hold a meeting or a discussion.

The leaders agreed on the need for a permanent church building to carry on more effectively with the ministry God was opening up there. They began having informal conversations with individuals in the parish, explaining the need and setting out the vision. Then they met with the members and then with the parish community as a whole.

One of the most impressive things about this parish is that everyone was taught from the beginning about stewardship and the responsibility to give. People were instructed that it was the parish's responsibility to support the priest and his family with a liveable salary, and that they could accomplish great things for Christ and his kingdom if everyone took ownership for the church's ministries, vision, and priorities.

People listened. Even more importantly, people began giving. The offering amounts went up radically. The parish board was careful to put the parish's money to good use and to be transparent in doing so. The time came when both the members and the leaders realized that their current facilities were too small to contain the vision they had as a church. They needed a new building. When the leaders began moving the membership in the direction of this major capital expense, they were both ready and enthusiastic.

> Everyone was taught from the beginning about stewardship and the responsibility to give.

But the leaders made a further decision, one that many people thought was crazy. In many other locations, churches wanting to build a building held out their hands to the bishop and pleaded for financial assistance. Sometimes overseas foundations or ministries provided funds. In both cases, the money was raised quickly, but the parishes and their individuals did very little to help make the church's new building a reality.

The leaders of this congregation, on the other hand, were concerned that such dependence upon outside funding might lead to a crippling attitude for years to come. They decided that no outside funding would be sought.

None of the members were wealthy. Not many had an education beyond high school. There were several businesspeople, some small shop owners, some who had small farms, and some who worked in town. So when the leaders laid the challenge before them, they gulped, and then they prayed.

Over the next year, a small miracle happened. The members gave sacrificially. The amount they needed to build the new church began to shrink. By the end of the year, the parish had everything it needed – while still paying the priest and covering the parish's normal expenses. People were astonished.

The new church building is big and beautiful. It has space for classes and meetings. The grounds look like a garden, with beautiful trees and flowers. The members are proud of what they were able to accomplish without outside aid.

But they are not sitting back and just enjoying their beautiful new church. Already they have several ministries reaching out to people in the slum communities down the road. They are also providing scholarships for students who otherwise couldn't go on to university. Now their even bigger dream is to build a Christian hospital. They own a big piece of land, and the church occupies less than half of it.

Is this an impossible dream for a church full of ordinary Christians? The members say no. They have already seen the miracles that can happen when they put their lives and their money in God's hands for him to use for his glory. When we free ourselves from the dependency trap, decide to depend on God, and give ourselves fully to his service, we can become part of accomplishing God's big dream for his world.

A "Poor" Church

Another church is in a rural area about a 45 minutes' drive from the capital. The parish was established in the 1980s. A grant from the denomination's central office enabled the new church community to purchase a piece of land that a neighbour offered at a good price. Another grant enabled the parish to put up a building of corrugated iron sheets on a wood frame.

The church numbered about 30 adults plus children at the time. Unfortunately, it has never grown much larger than this. Even though the congregation is small, there is a history of conflict and mismanagement on the part of former leaders. Pastors who have served this church consider this a difficult parish. It's not that the individuals are any worse than those found in other parishes. It's that the members of this parish don't give, and so the church never has resources to accomplish anything.

If anyone asks, the church members constantly say that they are poor and cannot afford to feed their families and give at the same time. However, it is widely known that several parish members own quite a bit of land, cows, goats, and chickens. They live in relatively comfortable houses. But the church building has never been updated in 30 years.

Not only that, but the church has also never even attempted to pay the pastor a living-wage salary. That is the denomination's job, they used to say. When the denomination's headquarters ran out of money to provide stipends for pastors, the church leaders steadfastly said: "We are too poor." Every week during the offering time, the members line up to put a small coin or two in the bag at the front of the sanctuary. When the money is counted at the end of the service, it is usually not even enough to cover the cost of serving a cup of tea to the people present.

As a result, the current pastor, a young married man with two small children, lives in poverty in the nearby city. The four of them live in one room. They share a water spigot and a drop toilet with 20 other families. Both the pastor and his wife are scrambling to take classes so they can find jobs to make a living. From time to time, one of the parish members will slip him some money to pay for transportation between the parish and the city.

When asked why no one contributes, members of the parish have said: "The denomination always paid for everything before, why should we pay now? This is *their* church; let *them* give us the money that we need. We've been crying for help, but they pay no attention to us."

> "This is *their* church; let *them* give us the money that we need."

Their ears seem to be deaf to any teaching about stewardship, about responsible Christian giving, about Christians' obligation to help the poor (which in this case includes their pastor!). They go along with what the church is doing, as long as someone else is paying the bill. They have excused themselves from any responsibility for so long that it has become their posture.

Sadly, this parish has become an example of a church that exists only for itself. They are deaf to who God is, and they are not interested in exploring what God might want them to be, what God might want to do in them and through them in the place where he has planted them. They aren't interested in reaching out to their non-Christian neighbours or helping other nearby churches in their own denomination with any of their projects.

When the current pastor suggested they could raise money for the church by starting a nursery school, the parish ignored his request for funds to do so, and the project died. When the pastor noticed that many of the neighbourhood children who came to services had not eaten, he undertook to have someone cook porridge for them every week. The pastor covers the cost out of his own pocket, despite his poverty.

Jesus says we can know a tree by its fruit. The fruit being produced by this particular church is not good. Instead, the parish is a classic (if extreme) example of what a spirit of dependency does to a church and its members. Their long-time behaviour reveals that they never understood the gospel, or what it means to be a disciple, to deny oneself, pick up one's cross, and follow Jesus. They have never understood, much less taken seriously the Lord Jesus's command to his disciples, "Freely you have received; freely give" (Matthew 10:8 NIV).

It is sad what these people are missing out on. Faithful pastors are leading services, but the good news of the gospel is falling on stony ground. Shrubs with no root will eventually wither and dry up, and in the end just be a bunch of dry sticks to use in the fire.

When the members of this local church claim to be poor, they speak more truly than they realize, for their hearts are impoverished and empty. If their hearts were instead full of God and the fruit of his Spirit, even the lack of material possessions could not stop them from becoming the most generous congregation in the country.

When we give God what we have, for him to use for his purposes, we open the door both to be his blessing, and to be blessed in return.

The Heart of Our Faith

Stewardship is the very heart of Christianity. It is the essence of a saving response to the gospel. Through stewardship, you and I say to the God who has so loved us: "This life you have given me is now yours to do with as you please. All these things and resources that I thought were mine are now yours."

Understood this way, stewardship has the power to transform every local congregation in the world. When churches understand the call to Christian discipleship and the call to stewardship, they do amazing things in people's lives and in their communities.

The medicine for what ails many struggling churches is the same medicine that Jesus himself offered so many years ago. It's the same medicine the apostles and the early Church Fathers distributed to everyone who would listen and respond. It's the medicine of basic discipleship, of making the choice to follow Jesus, to go where he goes, to do what he says, to be what he calls us to be.

Jesus warned the seven churches of Revelation 2–3 that they ran the risk of having their lampstands removed from their places. Think about that imagery for a minute. Imagine going to church for a service at night but finding it dark. Should we complain that we can't see to sing or pray? Should we blame one another for scheduling the service at night? No, we should realize that the building has been wired for electricity, that there are light bulbs in every socket, that all the connections have been made, and the power bill has been paid. All anybody needs to do is to stop grumbling and walk over to the light switch and turn it on. Then the church will be full of light.

We must not get so wrapped up in our own issues and petty arguments that we fail to notice our church has been built and wired and provisioned by Christ and that the Holy Spirit is with us and ready with more power than we could even imagine. We must not sit in the dark for so long we think it's normal.

May you have the courage to turn the switch on in your own heart, unleashing God's resources in your life. May you and your community become what Christ died and rose from the dead for you to become. May you and your church become what Christ poured out his Spirit at Pentecost for you to become.

It starts with being a faithful steward.

CHAPTER ELEVEN

Changed and Called

Now that we have learned so many principles of stewardship in our personal lives and our churches, it is tempting to think: "Okay, I have my to-do list. I can check these steps off the list one by one. As soon as I finish applying all I've learned from this book, I will be a great steward!"

Perhaps because I've mentioned how good stewardship builds trust and encourages congregants to give, you might even be thinking that stewardship is a programme your church can adopt to get people to give more money. While it is perfectly fine to think of ways to encourage people to give more, that diminishes stewardship to something much smaller than God is calling us to.

When we take these approaches, we treat stewardship as if it is a one-size-fits-all programme. Programmes can certainly facilitate many things, such as efficiency, or mobilizing people or resources. But creating a fail-safe programme is impossible. Many others have written and preached about stewardship, and if any one of their programmes had worked perfectly, we would all be using it. But stewardship, at least as Jesus and the apostles and the early church understood it, is not something that we can accomplish on our own strength, through our own tricks and tips. We can't become good stewards by grit and sweat. In cases where stewardship programmes have worked, it is because God was using a person to make a difference, running the programme for that time and place.

Christianity isn't about a programme. It's about a relationship between God and his people. The heart of stewardship is our relationship with God. How we each manage all that God has entrusted to us comes from each of our relationships with Christ. God has made every person different, and every church is different. Each church has its own well of human and financial resources. Each church has its own location and its own role to play in the advance of God's kingdom. But in every context, relationship with God will transform our lives and our perspectives. He will change our hearts, shift our priorities, and change our relationships with the people around us. Then God will use us to transform lives and churches.

Blessed for a Reason

God's call to be stewards is so different from the world's understanding that it requires a complete mindset shift. One of the biggest changes we must make is in how we understand blessing.

If what you have is God's property to give to others, you might ask: "Is there any blessing for me along the way?" Yes, of course. But not in the usual understanding of that word. All over the African countries where I have lived or visited, churchgoers are running after blessing. Everyone wants to be blessed. For many, this means financial prosperity, the ability to do whatever they want, to have whatever they want, to go wherever they want, to be whatever they want to be. In earlier times here on the African continent, blessing meant that my family and I were free from illness, that I had many children, that my sheep and goats and cattle were increasing in number, that my crops produced abundantly and there was no drought or famine, and that we were protected from curses. This certainly is an aspect of blessing in the Bible.

But the most important part is missing. In the Old and New Testaments, blessing doesn't come solely to be consumed by the blessed. When you or I receive blessing, we are then enabled to be God's blessing to those around us. This involves taking care of each other and also spreading God's blessing to people different from us. We are blessed to bless, as the Lord said to Abraham in Genesis 12:1-3:

'Go from your country and your kindred and your father's house to the land that I will show you. I will make of you a great nation, and I will bless you, and make your name great, so that you will be a blessing. I will bless those who bless you, and the one who curses you I will curse; and in you all the families of the earth shall be blessed' (NRSV-A).

This is the essence of stewardship, both in the Old Testament and the New. The world has always been eager for the blessing part. Many counterfeit versions of Christianity have pretended to have found the secret of unlocking God's blessing and prosperity for your life. But we are blessed to bless, not to be selfishly prosperous, as if prosperity were somehow a sign of God's favour, and not being prosperous a sign of God's curse. The apostle Paul, in his farewell message to the Ephesian elders, uses his own work as an example of giving everything one has in service of others:

'I coveted no one's silver or gold or clothing. You know for yourselves that I worked with my own hands to support myself and my companions. In all this I have given you an example that by such work we must support the weak, remembering the words of the Lord Jesus, for he himself said, "It is more blessed to give than to receive"' (Acts 20:33-35).

Christian stewardship is moving in a fundamentally different direction from the world's rush after blessing. We must be careful that Christian stewardship does not sink down into mere self-centredness. Like Ananias and Sapphira, we may think we can easily give a portion to God and hold on to the rest for ourselves (Acts 5:1-11). Through our giving and our prayers, we may try to manipulate God to get what we want. We can easily act like Jesus's disciples before they understood what Jesus was teaching, trying to force Jesus into our own presuppositions and expectations about money, leadership, spirituality, or the purpose of his kingdom (Mark 10:35-45).

When our mindset shifts to being stewards, we are no longer concerned about how much or how little we have. We realize that everything we are and have belongs to God. We give thanks that God has blessed us and entrusted us with these gifts. Our lives consist of managing what God has given in ways that help us to love God with all our heart and enable us to love our neighbour. It's not about being blessed but passing on God's blessing to others. Stewardship is that simple – and that challenging.

A Fresh Start

If stewardship involves leaving behind everything our world has told us about blessing and totally changing our mindsets, it's clearly not a programme we can accomplish with a few quick steps. Becoming a steward may seem completely impossible! And if we had to transform ourselves with our own strength, it would be.

It is hard for us to become stewards by trying to paint over our old life with a new coat of Christian ideas, language, practices, and postures. We can't just change the outside. We need an inner transformation. Becoming stewards requires beginning a new life, starting with Christ as the foundation for everything God wishes to do in and through us. This is why stewardship and discipleship are so closely related. In fact, from God's perspective, they may even be the same thing.

Jesus gives us this fresh start when we are born again (John 3:3 NIV). Jesus has died for us, and our old lives have died with him. So now we live our new lives for him: "He died for all, so that those who live might live no longer for themselves, but for him who died and was raised for them" (2 Corinthians 5:15). Our old selfish mindsets and values are gone. "So if anyone is in Christ, there is a new creation: everything old has passed away; see, everything has become new!" (2 Corinthians 5:17). Jesus promised to give his followers the Holy Spirit to enable them to follow him.

I owe my early Christian experience to the charismatic movement. But I have lived long enough to realize that the biggest miracle that the Holy Spirit works in someone's life is not speaking in tongues or prophecy or healing; rather the biggest miracle that the Holy Spirit has been sent to accomplish is to transform us and make you and me more like Jesus. On the last day, Jesus won't care what miracles we worked or how many demons we may have cast out or whether or not we speak in tongues. He does care passionately about whether we have become like him and have been concerned to give our lives to do his Father's will (Matthew 7:21-23).

When God's Spirit is present and working in our hearts, he gives us a hunger and thirst for God's Word. As we read the Bible and hear God's teaching, we realize these are not just words and stories on a page, but they are applied by his Spirit to our lives and circumstances. We become eager to listen to preaching or teaching. We want to know what the Word says and what it means.

With understanding comes conviction. We realize we need to change. God begins to reorient our priorities around his. Every repentant, born-again, Spirit-filled disciple and steward of Christ becomes a life-changing invader on behalf of God's kingdom, or God's new creation in this fallen world.

So for the genuine Christian, stewardship, like discipleship, comes naturally, naturally in the sense that this is what the Holy Spirit *wants and intends* to work in us. It's not a change we have to create in ourselves, like trying to swim upstream. It is where the river of the Holy Spirit is carrying the small boat of our faith, and the ship of our church.

Transformed to Transform

This same transformation happened to Jesus's first followers. They put off their old lives and were born again as new creations. They received the Holy Spirit. The change within them changed the world forever. And it was reflected in the way they practised stewardship. Take a look at this description of the church in Jerusalem in its early days:

> Now the whole group of those who believed were of one heart and soul; and no one claimed private ownership of any possessions, but everything they owned was held in common. With great power the apostles gave testimony to the resurrection of the Lord Jesus, and great grace was upon them all. There was not a needy person among, for as many as owned lands or houses sold them and brought the proceeds of what was sold. They laid it at the apostles' feet, and it was distributed to each as any had need (Acts 4:32-35).

> They took Jesus's call to be stewards and disciples seriously.

The early churches took Jesus's word seriously. They became known because of their stewardship and care for the poor. Their testimonies remain after all these years for anybody to read.

It's easy for us to find excuses for why we can't follow Jesus the way that the early church did. Many people in our churches may not know where their next meal will come from. When they pray in the Lord's Prayer for our Father to "give us this day our daily bread" it is for them not an empty phrase. It's easy to pass off this responsibility to some wealthier persons among us or outside donors. But let's compare ourselves to these early Christians for a moment.

The early Christians of the first, second, and third centuries had their issues, such as constantly struggling with false teachers. But they had none of the advantages that we have as Christians in most of Africa. In many countries, we have freedom of worship; they were periodically persecuted because it was illegal and considered subversive to be a Christian. We have TV, radio, internet, smartphones, and print publishing to help us get our message out; they had hand-delivered letters. We have vehicles, roads, and air travel. Their transport was by foot or using animals, and travel by sea was fraught with danger. If we consider ourselves to be relatively poor, or from poor, under-resourced countries, these people were, for the most part, poorer than we are, with no access to medical care, subject to the whims of weather and disease.

And yet, the Christian churches of the first three centuries grew and expanded so much that even empire-wide persecutions could not stop them. By the time Constantine became emperor in the fourth century, Christians were in the majority in many places, and paganism was in serious decline.

Why did the early church triumph? There are many factors feeding into a full answer to this question here. But at the top of the list is simply that they took Jesus's call to be stewards and disciples seriously. They were not, for the most part, interested in monetary gain or counting congregants. They weren't following Jesus because

Christianity was popular, or a place where rich and powerful people could be found. They were following Jesus because they had come to know him and knowing him was changing everything for them. It's these simple people, responding to the call to be disciples and stewards, who God used to change the Roman world.

We might ask ourselves, what has changed between then and now? Has the fact that the church exists in a hostile, unfriendly environment changed between then and now? Has the gospel changed since the apostle Paul was making tents, writing letters, and being persecuted in every town? Not at all.

In fact, throughout this book we have looked at stewardship from the Old Testament through to the early church. We have opened our Bibles and seen for ourselves that stewardship and discipleship are at the heart of Jesus's teaching. We have seen God's people responding to his call right up into our present day on our own continent. God is still calling us to follow him, to give everything we have and are for his glory.

Becoming a Christian is responding to Jesus's call to follow him as his disciple. Discipleship means stewardship, and both mean a transformation of one's life, priorities, and direction. When we respond to Christ's call to be his steward and his disciple, we follow him down a very different path than the easy Christianity that is currently trending in our churches. Our churches begin to make a difference in their communities. Our churches become communities of disciples and stewards, who with their gifts and service become the body of Christ where they are – the presence of Jesus in our communities.

We Can Be Stewards Today

Jesus is the same today as he was yesterday, and he will be the same tomorrow (Hebrews 13:8). The Holy Spirit who filled the church on Pentecost and empowered them to give themselves fully to serving God is the same Holy Spirit who fills us today. So God can do the same thing with me and you and our churches that he has done before. I have seen what can happen today when followers of Jesus take his call seriously.

Some years ago, I became familiar with a wealthy congregation in a university town. It had started as a small group unhappy with their previous church, specifically with the corruption of their leaders and the complacency of their fellow church members.

The church attracted people with its biblical preaching and through the members' outreach to unchurched friends and neighbours. The church realized they would soon outgrow their location. The leadership made a radical decision. Many churches would have built a larger building to house their growing congregation. But this church decided to multiply their church by preparing 200 members over the course of a year to establish another congregation in a different part of the town or in a neighbouring community. They trained their leaders and sent out their members.

The first new church was an immediate success and began drawing in people from the surrounding neighbourhoods. The mother church was so encouraged by the results that they did this again and again. To date they have established six thriving congregations where hardly any meaningful Christian witness existed before.

Yes, the mother church missed their former members. They prayed regularly for God's blessing on the new congregations. But as they continued their own outreach and mercy ministries, they continued to grow. For over twenty years they have held to their original vision of multiplying their church, and they continue to be God's blessing in that city.

They may not look impressive compared to the megachurches nearby who have enormous buildings and crowds of well-dressed people flowing in every Sunday. But this college town church has a huge impact for the gospel. Instead of spending their resources on their own comfort and prestige, they have prioritized increasing the witness of Christ in their area. It all started because the members have taken seriously their call to be disciples and to participate in the advance of the Kingdom of God in their town. Their commitment to discipleship drives their vision, and their commitment to stewardship makes it happen.

Sowing with Tears and Reaping with Joy

So what is our part in the journey to becoming good stewards? If it's not about our efforts but the Holy Spirit working in us, do we have any role to play?

One of the most memorable Old Testament images is a prophecy of blessing for the exiled remnant of Judah returning from captivity in Babylon:

> May those who sow in tears
>   reap with shouts of joy.
> Those who go out weeping,
>   bearing the seed for sowing,
> shall come home with songs of joy,
>   carrying their sheaves (Psalm 126:5-6).

The words are few, but sweet. For many societies in biblical times, the time of sowing was often a lean season. The previous year's harvest and supplies would have been running low, and there would be nothing to replace the dwindling food stocks. If the previous year's crop had gone poorly, your family and the whole community might be facing disaster. You might have had to take some of the precious remaining grain and commit it to the earth rather than use it for food. Hence the image of planting with tears.

But that is what brought the harvest with the great joy of sheaves of grain gathered into the storehouse. The whole community would have been relieved as they experienced God's provision.

Stewardship is like sowing. Christians must trust that God loves them. Christians must believe that God keeps his promises to provide for his people. Christians must choose to take Jesus seriously when he says, "Seek first his kingdom and his righteousness, and all these things will be given to you as well" (Matthew 6:33 NIV). Christians must determine that choosing the security of God's side and giving themselves completely to God's agenda is better by far than choosing to compromise and getting involved with the world's side.

In the reality of our lives, things may not look so black and white. We may face opposition or ridicule. It may appear that the world's side is winning. And it might feel as if God is far away, or absent altogether. This is not unlike when a farmer sows seed. Nothing happens. Days go by. But the experienced farmer knows that this is what happens with seeds. They get put into the earth, and they just sit there.

> Christians must believe that God keeps his promises to provide for his people.

But science has shown us that seeds are undergoing an immense transformation on the inside, getting ready to explode the hard shell and take on an entirely new, different, and immensely productive life. When the seed is ready, all it usually takes is a little bit of rain, and then it explodes.

The farmer notices some tender green shoots poking up through the earth. He cannot see that, underneath, each seed is sending out a root to tap into the moisture and nourishment in the soil. What used to be a seed now becomes a factory, transforming water, minerals, and nutrients into roots, stems, and leaves, using the sun's power to produce food for the rapidly expanding number of cells that make up the growing plant.

This is similar to what happens when we human beings get rightly related to God through our repentance and forgiveness that comes to us through Christ's death on the cross. Jesus says, "Very truly, I tell you, unless a grain of wheat falls into the earth and dies, it remains just a single grain; but if it dies, it bears much fruit" (John 12:24). The call to stewardship is ultimately not a call to success, or to blessing, or to happiness. It is a call to die. There is a solution to the problem in our hearts and in our churches, but it will cost us everything we have. "I am the way," says Jesus. "Follow me," says Jesus. "If any want to become my followers, let them deny themselves and take up their cross and follow me" (Mark 8:34). This is the decision that everyone who wants to be a Christian must make. Jesus is asking us to surrender our self-centred lives and trust God, putting everything back into his hands for him to use for his glory.

The cost may seem too high. But when we consider the alternative, Jesus's way to life always wins out over our world's way to death. Jesus calls us not only to die to the calls of this world, but also to be raised to new life. A life that now belongs to God. A life that's free to follow Christ. A life that's free to be God's partner as he reclaims his world. A life that is free to become God's blessing to the church and to those around each of us.

The question simply is, am I willing to follow Jesus? Am I willing to trust Jesus? Am I willing to sacrifice everything that I am and everything that I have? Am I willing to do what he wants me to do? Am I willing to go where he wants me to go?

In our partnership with God, it's not a 50%-50% arrangement. Instead it's 100%-100%. We give everything *and* God does everything. It's the same principle Paul describes with respect to our salvation in his letter to the Philippian Christians: "Work out your salvation with fear and trembling; for it is God who is at work in you, enabling you both to will and to work for his good pleasure" (Philippians 2:12b-13). In stewardship, we give back to God what was already his to begin with. We give it all, because it is his, not ours. We give it for him to use for his glory, because he is the owner of it all, and we are simply managing what is his under his direction. When we do, we come alive. We glimpse the harvest with joy. It was all worth it!

Called to Love

As we take our call to be stewards and disciples seriously, we become more like Jesus in our lives and relationships. We develop more and more of Jesus's heart and see the world around us through Jesus's eyes. Our hearts begin to fill up with the love he has for the poor and the lost.

Jesus calls his followers to love each other, in the same way that he loves them. Love is the engine that drives stewardship. This is not the love that most people in our day assume, a love that is often equated with satisfying one's sexual desires, or with affirming someone's choice to behave in a self-destructive way. Rather, love as Jesus practises it is self-giving. Love stops and helps, even if it is inconvenient. Love gives quietly, without attracting attention to itself, to help someone needy. Love takes time with the widows and orphans, feeds the hungry, visits the forgotten in prison, and cares for the sick and dying. Love intentionally mobilizes what we have and who we are for the sake of another.

One of the most influential prayers a person can pray is to ask, "Lord, open my eyes. Help me to see the people around me as you see them. Help me to love the people around me as you love them." This is a prayer that expresses the core of what God intends his salvation to do in our hearts (along with loving him with all our hearts). And it is a prayer that God loves to answer. This is a prayer that we stewards pray as we are seeking the Lord's will about what to do with our time, with our things, and with our money.

God will answer prayers like this, coming from the hearts of men and women who love God and want to love their neighbour. When he does, our churches will change. They will exist no longer just for our benefit, our entertainment, or our comfort. Instead we will see that our reason for existence is to become the love of Jesus where we are.

We can only love in community. So it is of vital importance that we are in a church community of like-minded disciples. Just as a seed needs the right conditions to grow, it helps for us to find a community where we can grow spiritually and become more and more like Christ. Perhaps you need to join a church where people are excited about following Jesus wholeheartedly. If you are a church leader, perhaps you need to find other church leaders and encourage each other as you lead your churches into becoming that community. Within the body of Christ, we grow in our commitment to stewardship, to following Jesus in every aspect of our lives. We then become the churches where the Kingdom of God is breaking into our world.

A Small but Caring Church

When love fuels our stewardship, God can do amazing things through us, the people who have become his partners.

I saw this in a very small congregation started by twenty or so members who were once part of a much larger parish in a nearby village. But because of the distance it took to walk to services, they first built a small chapel and secured the help of a retired priest who lived nearby. One of the members donated land and the others pooled their resources and built a small but suitable church.

The retired priest had noticed an unusual number of children in the area who were either orphaned or who came from troubled homes. It seemed there was nowhere for them to go for help, so he began to take them into his own home. Several members of the parish also saw the need and began to help by providing food for the old priest's growing family. When it became obvious that the priest's small house could not accommodate the six boys and girls who were now living there, members came together and persuaded a neighbour to donate more land adjacent to the church. On this land the members constructed two new houses plus outhouses and a kitchen. During this time, motivated by the priest's example, the church essentially began to understand these children not as the priest's ministry, but as the ministry and responsibility of all of them. The number of children began to grow.

Sadly, the old priest became ill and died. But his son took over and is now running the orphanage for the church, making sure the children are well fed and clothed and are going to school. Currently 16 orphans are living in the orphanage at the church. On Sundays, the little church is crowded, not just with members and friends, but with the children from the orphanage next door.

Already the church realizes that if they are to accommodate the people in the community who are already attending as well as any more children who come under their care, they need a more permanent building. So they have begun raising the money to build a stone church. The cornerstone has already been blessed and laid, and the congregation has been able to raise enough money to build the foundation.

None of the church members are particularly well-off. Most of them are simply farmers with small holdings. But they have a vision of how God wants to use them, and they have given themselves to that end. They have raised the money they need from their own resources. They aren't perfect, but they are a beautiful picture of what God can do when men and women willingly give themselves and their resources to God for him to use for his glory.

When the Holy Spirit gets hold of us, things don't stay the same. We see ourselves from God's perspective, and we repent. We see the church from God's perspective, and we feel a new sense of calling and mission. We see what we are and what we have from God's perspective. We begin to display Christ's presence in our community. Self-centred Christians or self-centred churches hardly become people and communities that are free to be what God is calling us to be. *We* become the blessing that God wants to pour out in the lives of the lost, broken, addicted, and poor. This is not something just for leaders or for ministers. We are all called to be stewards.

> We see what we are and what we have from God's perspective.

God is looking for people who have fully surrendered to him. God is looking for people willing to do whatever he wants them to do and go wherever he wants them to go. He will change our hearts and shift our priorities. Through his Holy Spirit, God will transform us into stewards.

He is calling us to love. To serve. To follow him. *God wants people who become his partners.* Are we willing to join in the joyful sacrifice?

Has reading *Raising Up Good Stewards* changed how you see finances?

The Radical Money Manifesto is perfect for your next church-wide Bible study. Invite your church members to learn what Jesus taught about money too!

oasisinternationalpublishing.com | oasisinternational.cor

THE RADICAL MONEY MANIFESTO: WHAT JESUS TAUGHT AND WE FORGOT
Joseph William Black

Based on the biblical and church history insights of *Raising Up Good Stewards*, *The Radical Money Manifesto* also includes Bible study questions for learning to be stewards together.

Jesus has a much bigger agenda for how you use the money he entrusted to you. It came from the Old Testament. It revolutionized the early church. Church fathers boldly lived it out in their communities.

Jesus issues a radical manifesto for citizens of the kingdom of heaven. He offers freedom from fretting, justice for the poor, and investment opportunities with eternal pay-offs. Whatever it costs, Jesus promises it will be worth it.

Order from oasisinternationalpublishing.com

oasisinternationalpublishing.com | oasisinternational.com

READ A SNEAK PREVIEW OF

THE RADICAL MONEY MANIFESTO

I need to warn you: what you are about to learn in this book could radically change your life.

You could find yourself with a fresh love for God and a love for others.

Instead of worrying about your finances, you might feel the lightness and freedom that comes from confidence in your Provider God. Instead of envying the rich, you might find yourself generously giving towards the poor. Instead of feeling guilty whenever the word *tithe* is mentioned, you might find a new warmth towards the God who has bestowed all gifts on you.

Does it seem strange that loving God and others more fully would be the result of a book focused on money? Those are the two greatest commandments in the Bible. Shouldn't they be discussed in a book about prayer or evangelism or something that sounds more ... spiritual?

And yet if you were to admit it, the word *money* might have been what caught your attention in the title. Because money is so important to us.

Too often, money occupies a place in our hearts that should be reserved for God alone. That's why Jesus talked so much about it. He said, "You cannot serve both God and money." That's why a book about money gets to the very heart of our relationship with God and with others. Sometimes, thinking money is not very spiritual is just an excuse not to let God touch that part of our lives. That is exactly when money is blocking us from a fully alive, transformed heart.

We need a radical solution: a new heart. As you will discover in this book, that is precisely what Jesus offers. It is drastic. Jesus calls people to take up their cross – or leave their fishing and tax collecting businesses – to follow him. The call is no less costly today.

And yet it is worth it. What land or bank or stock market offers investment opportunities with eternal payoffs?

This book's message is radical in another sense of the word too. While radical can mean extreme, it can also refer to roots and origins. As we delve into the Bible, we will discover a timeless message. During his ministry, Jesus laid out his manifesto for the Kingdom of God. In his parables and his famous "Sermon on the Mount", he described a bold vision for how we should live in relationship with God and others. He went back to the roots of the Old Testament law and explained God's original intent. It was radical. It sounded extreme. But really, it had been around since the very beginning, when God created humans as stewards.

The early church caught hold of this vision. Their generous community life can seem so shocking to us that we try to make excuses for why we can't live like that today. But when we look at the letters written by the early apostles and the writings of the Church Fathers, we see that they took Jesus's words seriously! These people heard Jesus's radical manifesto. They believed that being a citizen of the Kingdom of Heaven should impact how they responded to the injustice they saw in their churches and cultures. They did zealous things like standing up against corruption or selling their property and giving it to the poor. This was not just one or two people, but examples from centuries of church history.

Could it be instead that we are the ones who have lost our way?

I studied the Bible and church history and taught in seminaries and churches for a decade, frequently wrestling with the true meaning of Christian stewardship with my students. Looking around me, I saw confusion and hurt in our churches about wealth, money, and poverty. In Africa, everyday people miss salaries for months while gambling companies made fortunes. I saw orphanages who could not produce records of how they spent donor funds. I saw churches preach eagerly about one's duty to tithe, but not demonstrate the same enthusiasm to feed the hungry, care for the sick, or visit prisoners. I heard people compare pastors to police officers and politicians, all looking to line their pockets. I realized that in every case, we were not understanding the true teaching of Jesus on stewardship.

That is what motivated me to write a book. I wrote a book for church leaders, *Raising Up Good Stewards*, that tackles problems like dependency and false teachings about wealth and money. It gives practical advice on how church leaders can become more transparent and accountable. And it also delves into the biblical truths you will learn in this book. After I finished, my publisher said that this content was too important to tell only church leaders. Everyone needed to hear it.

The power of this book is not in my own words, but in the words of Jesus. We will encounter the testimony of God's people throughout the Bible and church history. As we do I pray that the Holy Spirit works his miracles of radically changing your heart and attitude about money the way he has done in my own life.

But this book isn't meant for you to read alone. When God gave the command to steward the earth, he gave it to Adam and Eve. When he gave the Old Testament law, it was to the people of Israel. When Jesus called his disciples, he called 12 of them to follow him together. So I encourage you that if you really want to be transformed, read this book with a community.

Find some friends, invite your small group, or ask your pastor if your whole church can read it together. Each chapter has a Bible study guide so that you can engage with the Scriptures yourselves. It has discussion questions for you to deepen your understanding and apply these truths to your lives. As you set aside time to meet in the next 10 sessions, I pray that the living God will work powerfully among you!

I can't wait for you to find out *What Jesus Taught and We Forgot*. I can't wait for you to swap duty for freedom, worry for gratitude, and envy for joy. I can't wait to see you on fire for Jesus, excited about the good news, and overflowing with love for your neighbour because of your new understanding of your calling to steward all God has given us. Shall we begin?

To order copies of this book for your group or to buy *Raising Up Good Stewards*, email orders@oasisinternational.com

About the Author

Dr Joseph William Black is a long-time missionary who has been training leaders for churches in Africa since 2000. His passion for stewardship comes from his experience serving churches in Ethiopia and Kenya, including pastoring the largest English-language church in Ethiopia. He brings a unique biblical and historical perspective on stewardship, with a BA from Duke University, an MDiv from Gordon-Conwell Theological Seminary, and a PhD in history from the University of Cambridge.

He has taught theology and history at several institutions in Africa, including the Ethiopian Graduate School of Theology in Addis Ababa and the Nairobi Evangelical Graduate School of Theology, now part of Africa International University in Nairobi. He is currently Senior Lecturer in Theology and History at St. Paul's University in Limuru, Kenya, and Senior Lecturer at Makarios III Patriarchal Orthodox Seminary in Nairobi, where he currently lives. He has previously published *Reformation Pastors: Richard Baxter and the Ideal of the Reformed Pastor* (Paternoster 2004) and many other articles on matters of history, theology, and missiology.

Acknowledgements

My life has been blessed and enriched by the input and examples of many people along the way, but two people stand out as particular examples to me of what it means to be a good steward of who they are and what they have. Father John Wangaru has been my friend here in Nairobi for more than a decade. I have watched him quietly give his time, his means, and his abilities to help the people in the parish, at the seminary, and at the monastery where he serves. I, too, have been in the circle of those so blessed. This is simply who he is, and he reminds me of Christ in so many ways. The second is Sister Photini (Megan Englebach) of St. Barbara Monastery near Santa Paula, CA. Sister Photini was a missionary at the seminary in Nairobi when I was assigned to teach here in 2015. She very graciously listened to my ponderings and complaints as I tried to get my mind around how our seminary students understood stewardship, or didn't, as the case may be. A lot of the ideas that became this book came out of our conversations. Her own commitment to Christ and her example as a good steward of all she is and all she has continues to challenge me deeply. Father John and Sister Photini, thank you for pointing me again and again to Christ. It is my prayer that this book may have the same effect on the ones who read it and take it to heart. Through the prayers of our holy fathers and mothers, Lord Jesus Christ our God, have mercy on us and save us.

Endnotes

1. Glenn M. Penner, "Dependency: When Good Intentions Are Not Enough" (Voice of the Martyrs, 2002), 3. http://www.vomcanada.com/download/dependency.pdf. Accessed 19 December 2020.

2. Roger E. Olsen, "Is the Prosperity Gospel Heresy?", *Patheos*, February 7, 2012, http://www.patheos.com/blogs/rogereolson/2012/02/is-the-prosperity-gospel-heresy/. Accessed 19 December 2020.

3. For an excellent resource into the many aspects of the Prosperity Gospel and the churches that utilize a prosperity identity and ministry strategy, see the 9Marks Journal, January-February edition, 2014, https://www.9marks.org/journal/prosperity-gospel/. Accessed 21 December 2020.

4. Kenneth Mbugua, "Misunderstanding the Bible," pages 15-32 in Kenneth Mbugua, Michael Otieno Maura, Conrad Mbewe, Wayne Grudem, John Piper, *Prosperity? Seeking the True Gospel* (Nairobi, Kenya: Africa Christian Textbooks Registered Trustees, 2015), 17-18.

5. Femi B. Adeleye, *Preachers of a Different Gospel: A Pilgrim's Reflections on Contemporary Trends in Christianity* (Nairobi, Kenya: Hippobooks, 2011), 61.

6. Adeleye, 105.

7. Although I use the word *covenant*, I am not talking about covenant theology in the way covenant theologians have understood it. My views on God's covenant with Israel at Mount Sinai, Jesus's ministry in the context of that covenant, and Paul's understanding of how Christ's death and resurrection affect those outside the covenant with Israel have been influenced more by a movement known as the New Perspective on Paul. During my time at Duke, I encountered E. P. Sanders and his book *Paul and Palestinian Judaism* (Philadelphia: Fortress Press, 1977). His work was furthered by the prolific and influential New Testament scholar, N. T. Wright. For those interested in learning more, I recommend:

N. T. Wright, *Paul in Fresh Perspective* (Minneapolis: Fortress Press, 2005).

—, *Justification: God's Plan and Paul's Vision* (London: SPCK, 2009).

Those who prefer to dive deep may enjoy his three-part series: *Christian Origins and the Question of God:*

—, *The New Testament, and the People of God* (Minneapolis: Fortress Press, 1992).

—, *Jesus, and the Victory of God* (Minneapolis: Fortress Press, 1996).

—, *The Resurrection of the Son of God* (Minneapolis: Fortress Press, 2003).

—, "New Perspectives on Paul" (lecture, Edinburgh Dogmatics Conference, Edinburgh, 2003). http://ntwrightpage.com/2016/07/12/new-perspectives-on-paul/. This lecture explains how and why Wright came to his position and his response to the controversy it has generated.

8   In addition to N. T. Wright, Prof. Meredith Kline also challenged my thinking regarding the covenant and prophets in his courses Old Testament Hermeneutics and Old Testament Prophets at Gordon-Conwell Theological Seminary, which I took in 1987-1988.

9   My original research discovered these different aspects of the Sinai covenant "tithe". I have since discovered others who have made the same point. See, for example:

Andreas Kostenberger and David A. Croteau, " 'Will a Man Rob God?' (Malachi 3:8): A Study of Tithing in the Old and New Testaments," *Bulletin for Biblical Research* 16, no. 1 (2006): 53-77, https://www.ibr-bbr.org/files/bbr/BBR_2006a_04-Kostengerger_Croteau.pdf. Accessed 22 December 2020.

10 For an overview of the issues around how Christians should relate to the OT law, see especially section 4 of:

N. T. Wright, "The Letter to the Galatians: Exegesis and Theology," in *Between Two Horizons: Spanning New Testament Studies and Systematic Theology*, eds. Joel B. Green and Max Turner (Grand Rapids, MI: Eerdmans, 2000), 205-36. http://ntwrightpage.com/2016/07/12/the-letter-to-the-galatians-exegesis-and-theology/. Accessed 22 December 2020.

11 Christians have often assumed we are obligated to keep the Ten Commandments. But in his letter to the Galatians, Paul assumes that the stipulations of the Sinai covenant could not be made obligatory for Gentiles without also forcing them to become Jews. Since the Ten Commandments are universally understood as the shorthand summary statement of the Sinai covenant, then it follows that Christians are not obliged to keep them, any more than they are obliged to keep the rules regarding circumcision, eating

kosher, festivals, fasts, tithing, etc. This does not mean, as some have charged, that Christians are free from the obligation to keep any law. Jesus, Paul, and James, to name a few, indicate that while the Old Covenant is obsolete, the New Covenant inaugurated by Jesus now defines our behaviour, morality, worship, discipleship, and stewardship as reconciled followers of the crucified and risen Messiah living in the new age of the Kingdom of God. Jesus radically redefined the source of kingdom morality when he told the Torah expert which were the two greatest commandments (Matthew 22:37-40). Christian morality is rooted in God's revelation of himself in the Old Testament but is now based on the way set forth by Jesus and the apostles (John 14:6).

12 The longest passage about tithes in the New Testament is Melchizedek receiving a tithe from Abraham in the Old Testament (Hebrews 7:8-17), which is in the context of the Old Covenant. Jesus also mentions tithes in terms of Old Covenant obligations. He points out the hypocrisy of Pharisees who are overly concerned (for example) to give a tenth of tiny bits of herbs while ignoring the greater requirements to love one's neighbour (Matthew 23:23; Luke 11:42). In another parable, Jesus mentions a Pharisee boasting about his own righteousness in prayer to God (Luke 18:12). Jesus is not interested in changing the *Torah* requirements concerning tithing (Matthew 5:17); rather he is concerned about demonstrating the hypocrisy of those who claim to be keeping the law (*Torah*) while their lives and relationships tell a very different story. Jesus came to make a new covenant, which includes a new understanding of stewardship. That is why no subsequent writing by any apostle or Church Father takes from this mention that we must therefore all keep the Sinai covenant laws with respect to tithing.

13 Irenaeus, *Against Heresies*, IV, 18:1, 2; emphasis added.

14 Thanks to Sister Photini Englebach for bringing this to my attention.

15 Lev. R. 34:8. Quoted in "Charity (Tzedakah): Charity Throughout Jewish History," *The Jewish Virtual Library*, last modified 2008, https://www.jewishvirtuallibrary.org/charity-throughout-jewish-history#2.

16 See my article, "Dependency, *Harambees*, and the Struggle for Christian Stewardship in the Orthodox Churches of Kenya" in *Pharos Journal of Theology*, 98 (2017), https://www.pharosjot.com/uploads/7/1/6/3/7163688/article_17_vol_98_2017.pdf. Accessed 25 December 2020.

17 The details of Anthony's life are told by the famous fourth-century theologian and persecuted Patriarch of Alexandria, Athanasius. Read more at https://christianhistoryinstitute.org/study/module/antony. Accessed 25 December 2020.

18 This story is summarized from Emmanuel Katongole, *Born from Lament: The Theology and Politics of Hope in Africa* (Grand Rapids, MI: William B.

Eerdmans Publishing, 2017), 202-219. Thanks to Hannah Rasmussen for bringing this story to my attention.

19. F. Scott Spencer, "Commentary on Acts 4:32-25," *Working Preacher*, https://www.workingpreacher.org/preaching.aspx?commentary_id=294. Accessed 26 December 2020.

20. John Holbert observes that Acts 4:32-35 in particular "has been characterized as either a rich call to a serious Christianity or the dangerous call to a life of socialism." He believes the passage should not be interpreted as a commentary on capitalism or communism. Rather, the early Christians' concern for the needy was how they bore witness to the Lord's resurrection.

    John Holbert, "Holding All Things in Common: Reflections on Acts 4:32-35," *Patheos*, last modified April 8, 2012, http://www.patheos.com/Progressive-Christian/Holding-All-Things-in-Common-John-Holbert-04-09-2012. Accessed 26 December 2020.

21. Jason Jackson is worried about association with 19th- and 20th-century Marxists. Forced redistribution of wealth, he writes, "is not a biblical concept. It does not represent the facts recorded by Luke and it does not conform to the sum of God's Word pertaining to these matters ... [For example] Not everyone received a distribution of what was laid at the apostles' feet. 'It was distributed to each as any had need' (Acts 4:35)."

    Jason Jackson, "Should Christians Have All Things in Common?" *ChristianCourier.com*, 2020, https://www.christiancourier.com/articles/1204-should-christians-have-all-things-in-common. Accessed 26 December 2020.

22. David Bentley Hart comes to a similar conclusion in his article:

    David Bentley Hart, "Are Christians Supposed to Be Communists?" *The New York Times*, November 4, 2017, https://www.nytimes.com/2017/11/04/opinion/sunday/christianity-communism.html. Accessed 26 December 2020.

23. John Holbert agrees. "Holding All Things in Common. Reflections on Acts 4:32-35," http://www.patheos.com/Progressive-Christian/Holding-All-Things-in-Common-John-Holbert-04-09-2012. Accessed 26 December 2020.

24. The word *deacon* is not used in Acts 6:1-7 to describe the ministry of the men who are chosen to help the apostles "wait on tables". Church tradition, however, identifies these men as the first members of the diaconate.

25. Rodney Stark, *The Rise of Christianity: How the Obscure, Marginal Jesus Movement Became the Dominant Religious Force in the Western World in a Few Centuries* (Princeton, NJ: Princeton University Press, 1996), 161-162.

26 Irenaeus, *Against Heresies*, IV, 18:1, 2; emphasis added.

27 The following quotations from the *Didache* are found at https://www.ccel.org/ccel/richardson/fathers.viii.i.iii.html. Accessed 27 December 2020.

28 Hadrian, quoted by John Ferguson in *Clement of Alexandria* (New York, NY: Twayne Publishers, 1974), 20.

29 Clement of Alexandria, *Who Is the Rich Man That Shall Be Saved?* William Wilson, tr., in Alexander Roberts and James Donaldson, eds., *Ante-Nicene Fathers*, 2 (Peabody, MA: Hendrickson Publishers, [1885] 1994), 595.

30 Clement of Alexandria, *Who Is the Rich Man That Shall Be Saved?*, 595-596.

31 Of Minucius Felix almost nothing is known. The date of his death is an estimate. He certainly predates Cyprian and may be a contemporary of Tertullian. All that survives of him is this one work, an apologetic dialogue between a Christian and a pagan.

32 G. W. Clarke, tr., *The Octavius of Marcus Minucius Felix* (New York, NY: Newman Press, 1974), 119.

33 Cyprian, *On the Lapsed*, 6. In A. Cleveland Coxe, Alexander Roberts, and and Sir James Donaldson, *Ante-Nicene Fathers*, 5 (Peabody, MA: Hendrickson Publishers 1994 [1886]), 438.

34 M. F. Toal, *The Sunday Sermons of the Great Fathers*, 3 (NP: CreateSpace Independent Publishing Platform, 2011), 331.

35 Ibid.

36 Ibid., 332.

37 See M. R. P. McGuire, 'De Nabuthae,' in *Patristic Studies*, 15 (Washington, D.C.: The Catholic University of America, 1927), 46-103l; see also Migne, PL, 14, 765-792, http://hymnsandchants.com/Texts/Sermons/Ambrose/OnNaboth.htm. Accessed 26 December 2020.

38 Ibid.

39 Augustine, *Expositions of the Psalms 121-150*, Maria Boulding, tr. (New York, NY: New City Press, 2004), 159-160.

40 John Chrysostom, *On Wealth and Poverty* (Crestwood, NY: St. Vladimir's Seminary Press, 1984), 49.

41 Ibid.

42 Ibid., 50.

43 Robert Holet reminds us: "The [Greek] term *oikonomos* (steward, house manager) ... appears frequently in the New Testament, particularly in parables where Jesus describes the 'servant' (disciple) as an *oikonomos*.

[The Eastern churches see its natural meaning as applied first to the church.] Orthodoxy also relates the term of *oikonomia* (stewardship) to that of *episkopos* – overseer, bishop, who is responsible for the oversight of the household of God (Acts 20:28, Titus 1:7, 1 Timothy 3) . . . [For the early Christians and] in Orthodoxy, the term *oikonomia* was never seen as strictly a matter of pragmatic management of personal or corporate financial affairs, but rather referred more broadly to the whole of human life and the manner in which Christian life is to be lived, the spiritual dimension being preeminent. As each Christian is to be a responsible steward, the bishop has the vocation to be chief steward of the local church. There was no sense of a separate 'theology of stewardship' in Orthodoxy, any more than there was a 'theology of ethic' or a 'theology of spirituality', rather Orthodoxy always focused on the multidimensional aspects of Christian life as a whole, of which what we call stewardship was an integral part." Culturally, the many different ethnic groups across the continent are much more holistic in their approach to life than their Western counterparts, so the early churches' holistic Christianity would likely resonate with most African Christians, if they knew such a thing existed!

Robert Holet, *The First and the Finest: Orthodox Christian Stewardship as Sacred Offering* (Bloomington, IN: Author House, 2013), 39-40.

AFRICA STUDY BIBLE, NLT
God's Word Through African Eyes

The *Africa Study Bible* is **the most ethnically-diverse, single-volume, biblical resource to date**. Written by 350 contributors from 50 countries, it includes the Holy Bible: New Living Translation, and more than 2,600 features that illuminate the truth of Scripture with a unique, African perspective.

The *Africa Study Bible* is a monumental study Bible, with notes by scholars and pastors in Africa who see the critical need to make Scripture relevant to our everyday lives. It's an all-in-one course in biblical content, theology, history, and culture.

"The Africa Study Bible *is a model of contextualized engagement of the Scriptures, with notes written by Africans, written for Africans, and answers Bible questions asked in African cultural contexts. It's a great encouragement to me to see such a resource available and I recommend it widely!"*
- *Dr Ed Stetzer, Executive Director of the BILLY GRAHAM CENTER*

Discover more at **africastudybible.com**

DOWNLOAD THE AFRICA STUDY BIBLE APP

The Africa Study Bible app is now on the Tecarta Bible App, the world's best study Bible app which is available to download on Google Play Store and Apple App Store.

OASIS INTERNATIONAL

Satisfying Africa's Thirst for God's Word

Our mission is to grow discipleship through publishing African voices.
Go to oasisinternationalpublishing.com to learn more.

INFLUENCE: LEADING WITHOUT POSITION
Philip E. Morrison & Hankuri Tawus Gaya
Do you have ideas for how to change your community, church, or nation – but feel powerless to make them happen? This book tells you how you can influence others to take action and start change, just as young men and women in the Bible did.

HIGHLY FAVOURED: OUR POWERFUL GOD'S COVENANT WITH YOU
Stuart J. Foster
The God of the Bible is not unreliable or inaccessible like the spiritual beings in African traditional religions. He chooses to have a covenant relationship with his people and we do not have to earn God's favour.

AFRICANS AND AFRICA IN THE BIBLE
Tim Welch
This book shows the presence and the participation of Africans in the biblical text, helping demonstrate that Christianity is not a "white man's religion" and that Christianity has deep roots in African soil.

AFRICAN CHRISTIAN THEOLOGY REVISITED
Richard J. Gehman
For all African Christians, *African Christian Theology Revisited* is a powerful plea to think through your faith in African contexts under the authority of the Word of God.

HELPING WITHOUT HURTING IN AFRICA
Jonny Kabiswa Kyazze and Anthony Sytsma with Brian Fikkert
This book trains leaders to proclaim the gospel in both word and deed, changing mind-sets and helping them apply biblical principles to care wisely and compassionately for people who are poor without unintentionally doing harm.

LEARNING TO LEAD
Richard J. Gehman
With its discussion questions and practical applications, this book will guide you to obtaining character and skills and help you become an effective Christian leader. It was written from the living experience of African leaders and it has been shaped by 36 years of training church leaders in Kenya.

ANSWERS FOR YOUR MARRIAGE
Bruce and Carol Britten
Offers practical insights to marriage issues and facts on sex, pregnancy, family planning, child-raising, money issues, adultery, HIV, and sex-related diseases. If your marriage is in despair, look to this book for some answers for your marriage.

PARENTING WITH PURPOSE & AFRICAN WISDOM
Gladys K. Mwiti
This practical guide for Christians is a relevant, thoughtful presentation on the characteristics of parenting that delivers results.

oasisinternationalpublishing.com | oasisinternational.com

SATISFYING AFRICA'S THIRST FOR GOD'S WORD

OASIS INTERNATIONAL
is devoted to growing discipleship through publishing African voices.

Engaging Africa's most influential, most relevant, and best communicators for the sake of the gospel.

Creating contextual content that meets the specific needs of Africa, has the power to transform individuals and societies, and gives the church in Africa a global voice.

Cultivating local and global partnerships in order to publish and distribute high-quality books and Bibles.

Visit **oasisinternational.com** to learn more about our vision, for Africa to equip its own leaders to impact the global church.

　oasisinternational.com　　oasisinternationalpublishing.com　　godswordforafrica.com

www.ingramcontent.com/pod-product-compliance
Lightning Source LLC
Chambersburg PA
CBHW060524080526
44586CB00012B/599